Destructive Politics

Destructive Politics

Government tampering with the economy gave us
every recession and depression in the past 100yrs.
Governments don't care who they harm!

Emil Szegner

Published: Self Published
Author: Emil Szegner
Copyright: pending
ISBN: 978-0-557-26909-9

Contents

☐ This Book is dedicated to our brave men and women in uniform; I thank you from the bottom of my heart for protecting us from evil. God bless your souls.

======================
Chapter 1 – Government
======================

"Those who are too smart to engage in politics are punished by being governed by those who are dumber." – Plato

The most powerful people in the United States are our leaders in the federal government. These are the people who write the laws we live by and create the departments that control us. Through laws and departments, the federal government determines our destiny and micromanages our behavior. During the past 100 years, our lawmakers have expanded their powers and have created 24 unconstitutional Federal Authoritarian Departments, which are actually controlling and restricting our freedoms and our rights to consume. Today, these controlling authorities are labeled as departments. Through departments, Congress regulates our lives from the amount of energy we can produce and consume to the taxes we pay on our incomes, electricity, and phone bills earnings and many other things. Government determines the rate of interest on our home loans, they also set mandates, fees, and levy taxes at will. The people in government who hold these powers in 2009-2010 are:

- the Speaker of the United States House of Representatives, Nancy Pelosi
- President of the United States, Barack Hussein Obama
- the Majority Leader of the United States Senate, Harry Reid.

Today, we are directly affected by every decision these three people make in Washington, D.C. This how ever goes back further, it actually started over 100 years ago when our leaders in the federal government started to ignored the constitution and began creating an environment through which handful of corrupt politicians would have total control over our lives. Over 100 years later, by the year 2009, our federal government has spent, wasted, and lost almost $13 TRILLION and that number is rapidly growing! With the help and support of the mainstream media, our government has been unstoppable at spending money and running up huge debts. This irresponsible behavior is directly affecting every part of our lives, from education, healthcare, affordable energy, social security, and mortgage interest rates, right down to the food we eat. Every single federal department in charge of our lives is mismanaged, corrupt, and counterproductive. They also cause the price of everything to be artificially higher than what they should be from energy, food, other goods and services. In the real world, supply and demand determines the value of a business, not a government authority. When someone makes a superior product, consumers buy it for the value and benefits it adds to their lives. The federal government does not believe in the principles of supply and demand. Thanks to ignorant leaders in the federal government, our economy has collapsed in 2009. Taxpayers have been burdened with a $13 trillion debt, which is increasing at an alarming rate. In Washington D.C. the government keeps creating more government, they think that is their job. If a department is corrupt or over budget, it doesn't matter; government just prints more paper money and issues more U.S. Treasury Bonds, selling out our future. Congress is so corrupt that they spend money until they see the need or create more need to spend more money. When they run out of money, Congress gets together and votes to increase funds so they can keep spending and printing more paper money. Through their destructive ways, our leaders are destroying free markets with bills like "Cap And Trade", Universal Healthcare, higher taxes, new federal departments, and more regulations. Without concern, they are driving our nation deep into debt and causing a recession and maybe soon a depression.

Every recession and depression this country ever experienced happened when the federal government started tampering with the economy and peoples wealth. They were able to circumvent the constitution and accomplish this through federal departments. These federal departments create an unpredictable atmosphere in our economy because the changes happen at the whim of corrupt leaders like Pelosi, Reid and Obama. Every four or eight years, we have a new administration take power and tamper with the jugular veins of our economy, manipulating energy and taxes. By tampering with these departments, they create problems, the kind of problems, which come to light many years later. When Pelosi passed alternative energy bills forcing us to use more bio-fuels, they also made it more difficult to get oil and coal. This caused a sharp rise in prices, which ruined a lot of lives. The government manipulation of the mortgage market, Fannie Mae and Freddie Mac, has been ongoing since the 1990s, also destroyed millions of lives all over the world. All this corruption and destruction can be traced back to the U.S. Congress and the likes of Rep. Barney Frank, Sen. Chris Dodd, and many others.

☐   Government corruption exists only because of the federal departments governments have created for themselves. They created these departments because they saw a lot of wealth created in the private sector. Once elected to office, politicians become greedy and believe it is with in their right to take a large cut of the profits from the people who produce and provide a service. Today, powerful politicians like Nancy Pelosi, Barack Obama and Harry Reid get their hands on people's wealth by creating additional fees and new taxes on industry. In federal departments, a few elected officials control trillions of dollars worth of wealth and commerce. The commerce politicians are manipulating and destroying happens to be the American people's lives and fortunes.

A handful of unqualified people heading these departments attract many lobbyists with suitcases full of money. Some of these lobbyists are retired representatives or Senators who return to Washington, D.C. in private jets with suitcases filled with promises to curry favor with the private interests they represent. Whether it's through campaign contributions or other forms of donations, the lobbyists always get what they need and want; it's just a matter of how much. This is corruption at its worst, and Congress is doing nothing to stop this. On any given Sunday political talk show, we can hear politicians on TV talking about getting rid of lobbyists and reforming Washington D.C. Yet nothing ever happens; lobbyists are still free to roam in DC and business continues as usual, each year more lobbyists than before. Why would this be? Most likely because these corrupt politicians receive a lot of benefits, votes and perks from lobbyists. Lobbyists come to Washington, D.C. because these

Federal departments exist. They come to influence the decisions Congress will make in all the departments, from energy and education to taxes and finance. The influence from lobbyists comes in form of campaign contributions or whatever else they may give. To put an end to this corruption and horse-trading, Congress should close all federal departments, reform the ones we truly need. Lobbyists will stop coming if we take away the reason for them to come. Closing all federal departments with the exception of Social Security and Medicare, we can solve all our financial problems. We will pay off the national debt and create jobs; freedom will once again reign across America.

☐

Today, the power to change Congress and the government (so it works for the people, not against the people) lie in the hands of The Speaker of the House of Representatives, Nancy Pelosi. Since 2007, when Nancy Pelosi became Speaker, her priorities were not to ensure a sound environment, in which Americans could prosper. Pelosi's plans were to change the direction America was heading with no consideration on how our economy would be affected. She did this through willful neglect by not meeting with the energy department and demanding they do all they could to increase domestic oil supplies. Instead, she passed bills in the house encouraging the use of bio-fuels. She did not consider how using food for fuel can destroyed the food market and damaged the environment. Nancy Pelosi single handedly caused the price of energy to double in less than two years from 2007 to the summer of 2008. This rippled through the economy causing millions of people to lose their jobs, homes, and retirement funds. Pelosi also did this to make Bush look like a bad president and ensure victory for the Democrats in the election of 2008. History tells us that what she accomplished helped Democrats get a majority in House and Senate and take control of the White House. The Democrats gained control of our nation through lying, cheating, and deceiving the American people while conspiring with the mainstream media.

☐

This is how politicians operate. They plan, scheme, and conspire to get as much power as they can get a hold of. Nancy Pelosi is proof. If you think about it, has any politician ever done anything to make your life better? Unless you are a trial lawyer, the answer is no. In fact, Washington politicians are the reason we are in the huge mess we're in. The mess is the recession of 2009-2010, our national debt, broken social security, broken education, expensive health care, welfare dependents, broken banks, foreclosures, and much more. Our leaders in Washington, D.C. have destroyed more lives with the stroke of a pen than any other group or organization in this country. This is the power government has over the economy. Now imagine how many lives they will take with Universal Healthcare! The private sector doesn't do near the damage to peoples lives as the federal government does. Sure, we can compare Enron to Fannie Mae and Freddie Mac. Which organization destroyed more lives? Fannie and Freddie are government-sponsored and regulated agencies, which are supposed to be under strict government scrutiny. Or are they? Fannie Mae and Freddie Mac's failures rippled around the world, bankrupted nations, and brought other nations to the brink of bankruptcy. It is true that Bernie Madoff is a criminal; the people whose lives he destroyed were devastated. Rep. Barney Frank, on the other hand, helped bring down Fannie Mae and Freddie Mac, costing taxpayers trillions of dollars. Bernie Madoff's losses were exasperated by the actions of the U.S. Congress, whose negligent behavior kneecapped the stock market. Thanks to Congress, the market lost half its value in less than two years. Not one person in Congress is going to jail or is being held responsible for causing the market meltdown. Rep. Barney Frank, Sen. Chris Dodd, Nancy Pelosi, among others were protecting Fannie Mae and Freddie Mac to the point where they blocked attempts to reform the ongoing fraud and corruption. The Bush administration attempted to reform Fannie and Freddie, only to be blocked over and over by corrupt Democrats. Some of these Democrats who blocked reform also received record amounts of political contributions from Fannie and Freddie.

☐

We are not asking for much from Washington, D.C. All we want is to ensure that the government does not become intrusive in our lives and we are not taken over by rogue nations. We expect a business-friendly environment so we can find jobs or start businesses without the federal government getting involved whether we are doctors, artists, entertainers, athletes, teachers, engineers, servers, plumbers, or any other honest professional. As long as we have a business-friendly environment, our economy will grow and provide jobs and other necessities in our lives without the need for a central government agency to regulate our behavior.

☐

Nancy Pelosi, Barack Obama, and Harry Reid are responsible for fixing all that is broken in government in 2009-2010. However, don't count on our problems being fixed anytime soon, for these are the people largely responsible for creating and prolonging the problems we are dealing with today. Our leaders are socialists who do not believe in the individual or the American capitalist system; they believe in unconditional central federal government control, like the old Soviet Union. They believe the federal government will bring us back the prosperity we had and deliver us to utopia.

In 2009-2010, as we look towards Washington D.C., we can clearly see Nancy Pelosi singlehandedly taking control of and destroying our free market healthcare. She pushed the mortgage market off a cliff by not allowing Americans more affordable energy in 2007, and she will force government healthcare through the House of Representatives and kill millions of Americans with ruthless government rationed health care. Thanks to Speaker Pelosi's neglect, Americans had to choose between food and fuel or paying mortgage and having no money for food or fuel in 2008. It is obvious (by the number of foreclosures) that most people bought food and fuel and skipped out on their mortgages. This imbalance happened because gasoline more than doubled in two years and Congress did nothing to stop this. Senator Reid repeatedly attacked the coal industry, which is responsible for over 60% of the electricity we currently use in our homes. Barack Obama lied and cheated his way to power partly by blaming oil companies for high prices at the pump and promising more unreliable green energy and jobs. Obama uses the oil companies as an excuse to convince us to buy environmentally hazardous hybrid cars and toxic mercury-filled light bulbs. As president, Obama's intention is to create a National

Socialist Government where the federal government controls banks, the auto industry, energy, healthcare, education, and any other important part of our economy. Our leaders, along with many others who are not as powerful in Congress, have been instrumental in bringing us the current recession and depression through which we are suffering. The three people listed below are the final decision makers in Washington, D.C. They have power to restore prosperity and jobs in America. They have the power to show the world the true power of free nations. These are the people who control our destiny!

	Nancy Pelosi, Speaker of the House (110th Congress)
	Barack Hussein Obama The 44th President of the United States
	Harry Reid Senate Majority Leader

☐　　There are many more names too many to list but the buck stops at the feet of these three. They are our leaders, and they have the power to reverse the direction in which we are heading. Their ideas and policies directly influence every single part of our lives, from affordable housing, affordable energy, affordable food, and quality schools, to affordable healthcare and jobs! YES, DIRECTLY! Make no mistake about it. These so-called leaders are touching everyone's life in this nation and the world. To see how irresponsible they are, just look at how everything is falling apart with no end in sight. When I say everything, I mean jobs are disappearing, homes are being foreclosed on, savings are disappearing, and lives are being lost. Everything that is important in our lives was tampered with by these three in Washington D.C.

If you were to ask the average American who these people are, outside of Barack Obama, most people have no clue. People don't know who Nancy Pelosi or Harry Reid is, nor do they know or care whom Barney Frank or Charlie Rangel is. When I say most Americans, I mean about 65% do not know who they are or how they have impacted their lives. On the other hand, if I were to ask most Americans to name the artist of a hit song or some other question about a pop culture icon, they would know the right answer and probably tell me something I didn't know. This is exactly the kind of environment that the Democrat party thrives on and helped crate, a nation of IGNORANCE.

☐☐

Whether it's pop culture, sports, or any other interest, most people are preoccupied with their lives and could care less about

Washington, D.C. There is a very good chance that politics is the furthest thing from their minds. They are not aware that the politicians touch every part of their lives like no others. Ignorant Americans are the very people voting for the likes of Obama, Reid, and Pelosi, the ones ruining all of our lives. These three people are true socialists with an untold amount of power over us via departments. The only way to fix our problems is to take away all the power they have over us. With no power over us, they will not be able to harm us with their plans of social architecture of our society. With no federal government manipulation of energy, banks, healthcare, manufacturing or salaries our nation will prosper more than it did under Ronald Reagan, God bless his soul.

□ □

Every American voter should know what policies Pelosi, Obama, and Reid advocate and how they will affect their lives. Voters should know that it was government neglect that caused the price of energy to more than double in less than two years under Pelosi's leadership. When she took The House of Representatives as Speaker, gasoline was around $2/gallon. Under her control, the price of gasoline rose as high as $5/gallon in some areas in California. Many Americas actually believed that it was the oil companies and speculators manipulating the prices. Even popular TV hosts like Bill O'Reilly believe that Big Oil and speculators are to blame for the rising price of energy. This couldn't be further from the truth. In fact, oil companies couldn't set the price of oil even if they tried. The price of oil is set in the free market. The oil market is global, meaning that the oil companies would have to have trillions of dollars to be able to manipulate the prices. They would also leave a paper trail a mile long to prove their manipulation in these markets. The oil companies had nothing to do with the price of oil going to $145/barrel, the same way the gold miners have nothing to do with the price of gold going over $1,000/oz. It's supply and demand!

□□

The supply and demand part of the market is the most logical and natural system in the world. The price of oil is purely dictated by how much oil we have in the market and how many people want to buy it! The sad thing is people are demanding more government oversight. This is INSANE! If you want government oversight in oil, just go to Europe. They pay over $6/gallon. That is the cost of government oversight. We just have to look back at the Jimmy Carter years to see the proof of government corruption in energy. Before Jimmy Carter created the Department of Energy, gasoline was under $1 a gallon in the U.S. After the Department of Energy, America had gas lines, and gasoline went over $1/gallon.

□□

When there is an imbalance in the supply of oil to one side or the other, the price will move accordingly. If we have too much demand but not enough supply, the price will rise until we bring more supply to the market. This is what happened in 2007/2008 under Pelosi's leadership. Our demand was on the rise, but Pelosi did nothing to increase the supply. This in turn ran the price of oil up to $145/barrel. In other words, if a company is selling goods and they need a certain amount of raw material to create those goods, but our government controls the access to the raw material and does not allow the company to increase the supply of that raw material to create those goods, the price of those goods will inevitably rise. Demand for oil was on the rise as more and more people were using energy. Nancy Pelosi purposely held back the supply of affordable energy by not lifting bans on drilling to increase domestic production of oil. Speaker Pelosi singlehandedly destroyed the American economy by limiting the flow of oil in 2007. She deliberately held back American companies from drilling for more oil in the U.S. American oil production was capped by Congress; the demand was on the rise and hardworking Americans needed more oil from the world market. The problem is, the rest of the world was also growing and using more energy. With supply tight and prices at the pump on the rise, millions of Americans had to use disposable income to pay for the higher price of gasoline. This was the break in the economy that started the recession/depression we are suffering through in 2009,2010.

☐

This is simple economics 101. This is exactly what happened in the energy markets, but for some reason, oil companies are the villains. Oil companies make money by selling oil and gas. Why would they hold back supply? The more they sell, the more they earn. Why on earth would anyone want to sell less of something if people want to buy more? By not educating our nation properly, we remain victims of ignorant Americans voting for irresponsible politicians who do not understand or care to understand how our economy and the free markets work.

Our leaders have destroyed our mortgage market, manipulated the energy market, and ruined public education, social security,

Medicare, and jobs for millions of Americans. Then they turn around and blame the free market for causing our problems. They attack CEOs, use unions, RentA-Mobs, ACORN, and other socialist groups to create havoc and get their point across. They organize and bus people into rallies from neighboring states using taxpayer dollars. These Rent-A-Mobs are made up of low-income people who are easily manipulated by Democrats. The Democrat party also uses organizations to pack crowds so people watching on TV believe that Americans, in large part, support socialist agendas.

Dishonest politicians like Nancy Pelosi have no problems using innocent Americans as pawns and stepping stones to get their government programs passed. That is exactly what she orchestrated to ensure a Republican defeat. The very person who had the chance to limit the severity of the market crash, real estate crash, and any other collapse happening now is none other than Nancy Pelosi. She had the power to stop it all, and she still has the power to put an end to rising unemployment, falling home prices, and rising energy prices. She has the power to reform Social Security, Medicare, and just about every other self-destructive government program under which we are forced to suffer. "So just who is Nancy Pelosi?" you may ask.

Our nation entered into a new era on January 4, 2007, when Nancy Pelosi became the first female Speaker of the United States House of Representatives in the history of the United States. It was indeed an historic occasion for women all over the world. Finally, a woman has become the most powerful person in the United States and possibly the world! But who is Nancy Pelosi and how did she get elected? Is she qualified and responsible to be Speaker of the House and in control of our nation and our lives? Who does she represent? Nancy Pelosi was elected in 1987 when her friend, former Congresswoman Sara Burton, fell to illness and died in office. Her dying friend, Burton, asked Pelosi to take her place, and ultimately, Pelosi was elected. "She was picking her successor," Pelosi said. "Men do it all the time." At the time, Pelosi was worried about leaving her teenage daughter at home, but when her daughter told her to "get a life," it made her realize that she could move on to other greater challenges in life. Why not become a representative in Congress?

Most people are unaware of how she was able to manipulate her way to the position of Speaker the most powerful position in the WORLD! How exactly did she get to that position? We need to look back to the fall of 2006, when Nancy Pelosi was the Minority Leader of the House. The biggest story was about to break all over the media. This story captured the headlines in October of 2006 and stayed in mainstream media reports almost every day until Election Day. What was this big news that required wall-to-wall coverage by our mainstream media? Was it the fragile state of our mortgage market? Was it the war on terror and the threats from extreme Muslims? Or was it the rising price of energy? No, the biggest story to break in the U.S. was the Mark Foley sex scandal. A Republican Senator was caught sending sexual text messages and emails to his pages (high school students who work with lawmakers). In concert with the mainstream media, the Democratic party led an all out attack on Mark Foley, and exploited his sex scandal in hopes of capturing more Democrat seats in the upcoming election. The media didn't start this attack when it happened in the spring of 2006. Together with the cooperation of the mainstream media, the story was held back until September and October of 2006. It worked! With the print and television media running wall-to-wall coverage of this incident, voters decided to vote for Democrats in the 2006 midterm elections, giving Democrats a majority in the House (Democrats never resign or get kicked out for sex scandals; they get promoted!). The sad thing is while the Democrats were manipulating and cheating the system to gain power, real, serious problems were brewing and slowly beginning to overflow.

□□

Trough trickery and manipulation, Nancy Pelosi and the Democrats gained control. Because of her leadership, Pelosi became Speaker of the House. She was ready to control.

"We will not just break through a glass ceiling, we will break through a marble ceiling," said Nancy Pelosi. "In more than 200 years of history, there was an established pecking order -- and I cut in line," said Pelosi.

She calls herself "the most powerful woman in America." Mrs. Pelosi flexed her right muscle like a bodybuilder to her socialist constituents and supporters at a gathering called a "women's tea."

"All right, let's hear it for the power," she screamed in delight.

Speaker Pelosi was no stranger to controversy. As Minority Leader of the Democratic Party, her mission was not the safety and security of the American people, nor was it fixing Social Security or Medicare, programs that are bankrupt. Her number one priorities were to take control of our country and to impeach President Bush. During her time as House Minority Leader, Pelosi was on a never-ending quest to destroy George W. Bush. The Washington post wrote on May 7, 2007 of the newfound confidence the Democrat leaders were feeling. They were planning an all out legislative assault against businesses by raising their taxes and increasing regulations. Under Pelosi's leadership, Congress became an obstacle in the war on Terror and the hunt for extreme Muslims hell bent on killing us. In an interview with the Washington Post, House Minority Leader Nancy Pelosi stated that the Democratic House would launch a series of investigations of the Bush administration beginning with the White House first-term energy task force and most likely including the use of intelligence in the run-up to the invasion of Iraq. She denied any suggestions that this was a move to attempt to impeach President Bush, but she did state, *"You never know where it leads to."*

After reading the Washington Post interview with Nancy Pelosi, one has to wonder where Speaker Pelosi's priorities lie. One thing is certain; she does not care one bit about taxpayers. When she became Speaker of the House in 2007, her number one priority was to have us use alternative bio fuels. She focused heavily on expensive alternative energy. Supplies were not keeping up with demand for energy, oil or gas. This negligence by Pelosi caused higher prices soon after. The higher cost of energy caused businesses to have to lay people off, causing unemployment to rise. Her goal was to ensure that the economy was in recession by the time Bush's term was over. Her third priorities were cover-ups for Democrat scandals, misuse of government powers, and splurging of taxpayer dollars. She was also hard at work silencing the opposition. All these things happened while Americans were busy living their lives, raising their families. Her path of destruction is clear and present and is all over the Internet, from You Tube to news articles. Everyone should get familiar with Nancy Pelosi; She has touched everyone's life in America since she has been speaker.

In the summer of 2007, our economy was beginning to show signs of serious problems. The mortgage market was starting to show signs of distress due to the rising price of energy, but that did not seem to matter to Pelosi. She did not take the appropriate steps to save the American taxpayers from this looming disaster she instead decided we should focus on alternative energy. Pelosi did not care how many jobs and homes were being lost month after month. She is a multi millionaire. As long as she gets her way in

Congress, she doesn't care how many lives she destroys. Millions of Americans simply became casualties of her tyrannical behavior. We are now living through the results of her actions, and the worst is yet to come. Many people already lost almost everything in 2007-2009—exactly what the Democrats have been planning. The leaders in Congress are not troubled by the American taxpayers' problems. They use us like chess pieces, boldly trying to predict our behavior as we sink deeper into recession. When it seems that all hope is lost, they promise desperate people prosperity through government interventions and more social programs. They proposed increasing unemployment benefits and bailing out banks. They want to provide healthcare for everyone by promising they will be honest and competitive. This is how Democrats lie and cheat their way to power. This is how they fool the unsuspecting among us and empower the federal government.

□□

The reason Pelosi will never stand up for Americans is that she belongs to the special interest groups first and foremost. The entire Democrat party belongs to special interest groups and lobbyists. The special interest groups and lobbyists are a mob of trial lawyers, ex-politicians, and union bosses who are only concerned about them selves. Once a Democrat is elected, they no longer serve the American taxpayer. They answer to special interest groups and the corrupt organizations that got them elected legal lobbying groups, union bosses, and other socialist groups like ACORN. The payback for the election of 2008 was a large amount of money in the stimulus bill of 2009 designated for ACORN. The payback to trial lawyers was no tort reform. The payback to unions was U.S.

government tarp money. Even though it has been proven that ACORN is a corrupt organization registering phony votes to the tune of over 400,000, attorney general Eric Holder still fights to ensure ACORN gets the federal in tarp funds. This is the same attorney general who liberated Puerto Rican terrorists in the 1990s when Hillary Clinton was running for Senate.

□□

The person who approved the stimulus bill of 2009 and rewarded ACORN and other criminal organizations was Speaker of the House Nancy Pelosi and her socialist Democrat allies. Instead of focusing on fixing Fannie Mae and Freddie Mac, when Pelosi took control of the House, she ignored them, our financial system, and our dire need for energy. Even before she became Speaker, the Republicans had been trying to fix Fannie Mae and Freddie Mac over and over with no success, as the Democrats ran the banking and finance departments. □

□

In 2005, U.S. Representative Ed Royce had an amendment backed by the Federal Reserve that would have reined in the risks being taken by the Government Sponsored Enterprises (GSEs) like Fannie Mae and Freddie Mac. The Democrats stood in his way and made sure that Fannie Mae and Freddie Mac would not fall under the scrutiny of strict regulatory oversight. Democrats blocked the reform of these GSE's. They were allowed to keep operating, as they were to ensure continued deterioration of our mortgage markets. Nancy Pelosi ignored all of this; as Minority Leader, she did not seem the least bit concerned. As soon as she became Majority Leader, she was more concerned about the flowers in Capitol Hill than the issues, which had to be dealt with. She was not concerned about the financial markets because the Democrats used Fannie Mae as their personal piggybanks! Over the past decade, Fannie and Freddie have spent nearly $200 million on lobbying and campaign contributions to politicians. At the same time, democrats portrayed Rep. Ed Royce's attempt to stop this grand larceny as an attack on homeownership and affordable housing. Looking back, it was unfortunate that America lost this battle. Had the Senate Democrats (with ACORN's help) not been able to block meaningful legislation from passing in 2005, Congress could have kept the GSE's from getting out of control, and our financial markets and the broader economy would be in far better shape than they are today.

ACORN has developed a lengthy history of voter fraud, which spans more than two decades yet democrats insist that ACORN receive federal funds. In the 2008 presidential election, ACORN was investigated in 14 states for massive voter irregularities. Even ACORN's allies were troubled by their actions. After the elections, the head of Project Vote (a left-wing nonprofit organization) admitted that over 400,000 newly registered voters by ACORN in its $18 million voter registration drive were rejected by state and local election officials as fraudulent. Nancy Pelosi used her powers to block all investigation of ACORN by Congress. When representative John Conyers dropped his investigation of ACORN, a reporter asked why. His response was, *"The powers that be decided against it."*

* when the most powerful people in the country order police not to

investigate election fraud, and over $4 billion of federal money is on its way to corrupt organizations, WE ARE IN TROUBLE. That means LAWS NO LONGER MATTER!!! If we do not abide by laws, we will be left with chaos!

Using organizations like ACORN, the Democrats were able to successfully steal many House and Senate seats in the 2008 election, including the Al Franken Minnesota election. These are the results democrats have been counting on, it's no surprise Pelosi would make sure ACORN received a large chunk of the stimulus money.

Most people have no idea how much impact Speaker Pelosi has on our lives and the price of energy all across our nation. When the price of oil was reaching $145/barrel in the early summer of 2008, Speaker Pelosi not only had the power to pass energy relief to bring down the price of oil; she had the obligation! People were hurting. We needed our government to lift the bans on drilling for oil in our own country. She could have instantly helped Americans by cutting the federal gasoline tax of 18.4 cents per gallon and lifting the ban on drilling for oil so we could have increased supplies. Just lifting the ban on domestic drilling would have bought the price of oil down to under $100/barrel and gasoline to the $2 range. To an average family, this would have helped a lot. Concurrent with cutting the Federal Gasoline Tax, she could have also proposed a bill to increase the domestic production of oil and gasoline and let the states decide whether they wanted the oil companies producing more. These are all meaningful steps that would have kept the price of gasoline down and unemployment low. The low prices on energy help taxpayers keep more of their income to pay bills and mortgages, and it would also have lowered the cost of food, family vacations, and just about anything else in people's everyday lives. Those are the kinds of changes, which create jobs, wealth, and prosperity. Low taxes and small government is what makes our economy grow! Unfortunately, that was not Speaker Pelosi's priority. She found more important things to worry about than the American taxpayers' lives. Upon becoming Speaker, one of Pelosi's first orders of business was to have more flowers in the Capitol about $16,000 worth more per year. She spent, twice as much money on meaningless cosmetic things as her predecessor Denis Hastert.

□□

While Pelosi was on her spending spree, the price of gasoline was rising week by week. People were watching their disposable income disappear. Instead of going on vacation, going out to dinner, or splurging on a cup of eight-dollar coffee at Starbucks, people stopped spending and started cutting back on luxury items. While people's lives were falling apart, the person who holds the power to change this, Nancy Pelosi, was busy arranging the flowers in the Capitol Building. But that was not the only thing on Speaker Pelosi's order of business; she was also steadfast on updating the House lunch menu. Yes, she didn't care if you could feed your family; she cared about updating the menu in Congress's mismanaged cafeteria. She added organic food to the menu. Instead of outsourcing to successful franchises that could get the job done for a fifth of the cost of what it takes government to do it, she decided to waste more of our tax dollars on government-run inefficiencies. She was not finished yet; she still had very important items to deal with. While the price of energy was still rising and mortgage delinquencies were starting increase, she found it important to tease us by promising a vote on the energy bill, only to change her mind the next day. She did this on more than one occasion in the summer of 2008. She also used her position as Speaker to splurge on taxpayer-funded travel for her family and friends. On top of all that, she uses her power as Speaker of the House to ensure favorable bills for her constituents.

On January 12, 2007, The Washington Post wrote about how Speaker Pelosi sneaked a provision to exempt her district and the U.S. territory of Samoa from the minimum wage increase. This was done directly to ensure her constituents at Star-Kist Tuna Co. did not have to suffer the higher costs of production like the rest of the nation. House Republicans brought this up on the floor on August 7, 2008. When members questioned the provision in the minimum wage bill which not only exempted Pelosi's district from the increase in the minimum wage, but also from stem-cell research a clearly angered and out of control Barney Frank screamed at the top of his voice and hammered his gavel to silence and squash the opposition. Why would she exempt Samoa and her district from the minimum wage bills? Pelosi's district happens to be the home of Star-Kist Tuna Co., owned by Del Monte Corp. They are headquartered in San Francisco, which is represented by Nancy Pelosi! Whom exactly is Pelosi trying to protect?

No matter how bad things were getting, how low the Congress approval rating was drifting the Democrats did not care. They don't care if you lose your job, your house, your retirement, or anything.

Once they have your vote, you can just drop dead as far as the Democrats are concerned. They will still get your vote whether you are dead or alive; it doesn't matter. Many dead people have been voting Democrat all over the country for the past 50 years.

□□

Pelosi is a self-destructive force in the Democratic Party and in our nation. To find proof, we need to look at Congress's approval rating before Pelosi came to power. Congress enjoyed a 38% approval rating before Pelosi took over. In just two short years, the Democratic Congress led by Nancy Pelosi cut their approval rating to just half of what it was before she took power as Speaker. The current 2009 approval rating is below 18% and still falling. She doesn't care! Her priorities were to attack and discredit the Bush administration at every step. She kept teasing us that she would introduce an energy bill, only to change her mind OVER AND OVER. Instead of keeping the economy from falling off a cliff, she focused on her book tour, which kicked off in early August of 2008. While on her book tour, people were protesting across the street from Borders book and music store. Taxpayers were standing in the rain with signs demanding more energy, more oil, and more gasoline. Ignoring hardworking Americans, she decided to focus on her book and her ignorant audience in the bookstore. She was asked questions about her book and lessons for daughters and women. "It's more wholesome when there is more diversity at the table," Pelosi said, "and nothing has been more wholesome than including the participation of woman at the table." Meanwhile, protesters were getting soaked outside with signs demanding she do something about the price of energy, for only Nancy Pelosi had the power to help reduce the price of gasoline. SHE DID NOT CARE! □□

She felt it more important to promote her book and forget about the energy issues and the financial meltdown that was just around the corner. The stock market and economy started to melt down about five weeks after she kicked off her book tour. How much more do people have to see to understand that Nancy Pelosi does not care about Americans? She purposely stood by and let everything fall apart, and she felt no remorse whatsoever. She is the one person who can change it all! In Nancy Pelosi's world, if the price of energy does not affect her constituents or her family, then she does not care about it. Besides, she is a member of Congress. She doesn't have to pay for anything! We pay for her!

□

To truly understand the arrogance and elitist attitude this woman possesses, we need to look back to the Democratic Convention in the summer of 2008. On her way into a meeting demonstrators regarding energy once again greeted her. These demonstrators were hardworking Americans, directly affected by the high price of gasoline. Together, they chanted, "Drill here! Drill now!" in hopes of Pelosi taking the energy policy seriously and increasing domestic production of oil. She still didn't get it. Instead of doing the right thing and working on energy, she paused and mocked the protesters by saying, "Right here?" With a smirk on her face, she seemed to take pleasure in these people's pain and misfortune and yelled out, "Can we drill your brains?" Like the rest of the arrogant, elitist Democrat leaders, Pelosi insulted the American taxpayers who were just trying to get a break!

She continued by referring to the protestors as "handmaidens of Big Oil." She then argued that increased offshore drilling would reduce gas prices by only a couple of pennies a decade from now. She then started referring to the crowd as the "two-cents-in-ten-years-crowd."

☐

Steny H. Hoyer, the Democrat Majority Leader in the House, also took a jab at the demonstrators, saying "sophomoric chanting" would not change the energy crisis and that "all thinking Americans know." This blithering jewel of ignorance had the audacity to continue bashing the protestors by trying to convey false facts "that America doesn't have a quarter of the word's fossil fuels, yet uses a quarter of the world's energy." ☐ That statement is 100% FALSE! American has more oil than the Middle East! We are not permitted to get it because Nancy Pelosi, environmentalists and lobbyists have hijacked our nation! Make no mistake; the oil companies did not hijack our nations. The socialists, communists, and lawyers have taken over and are robbing our nation of a bright future.

☐

Pelosi's efforts were calculated and destructive for the purpose of making George W. Bush's last few months a disaster. By not focusing on Fannie Mae and Freddie Mac, which were under the strict oversight of the House Banking committee, Speaker Pelosi instead focused on cosmetics like Flowers and lunch menu. Her actions alone exacerbated our financial melt down, which reached all over the world. Many foreign nations purchased mortgage-backed securities from American Investment Banks. These banks sold Mortgage Backed Securities to investors all over the world. FannieMae and FreddieMac backed many of the securities giving the appearance that they were safe investments. People around the world had no idea these loans were given to unqualified borrowers with no hopes of repaying the loans.

Pelosi didn't do all this destruction alone; she had her loyal supporters doing the dirty work in the background people like Barney Frank, Chris Dodd, Chuck Schumer, and many other corrupt Democrats. While the world was falling under the spell of Obama, the real culprits were hard at work destroying our banking system, blocking energy, and ensuring a path to socializing America.

□□

Everyone seems to think Obama is the one in charge. However, Obama does not set policies, work on new laws, or expand government. It is Nancy Pelosi who heads closed-door meetings about controlling and manipulating people's lives by way of government departments. Obama is more like the cheerleader, he comes out to read the teleprompter when his controllers are ready to push an agenda bills like cap and trade, the closing of Guantanamo, government healthcare, cash for clunkers, or other bad government ideas. The person in charge of our country, the one deciding our faith and future for all, is the Speaker of The House of Representatives, Nancy Pelosi, and the socialists who follow her leadership. Pelosi runs the Capitol like a ruthless dictator. She covers up crimes and unethical behavior by people in her party.

During the budget and tarp talks, she flexed her political powers by not accepting any of the ideas presented by the Republicans. In fact, in an interview, when asked about Republican input to the healthcare bill, her response was, "They were there!" They were not allowed to have any say in the bills; they were just allowed to sit there and shut up. In January 2009, she tried to rewrite the rules in the House so the Minority Republican Party could not stop her socialist agenda. Fortunately for America, she failed. Pelosi is ruthless and unforgiving; she wants total control over our lives! She will not stop her quest for ultimate control until she gets her way! We can hear her words almost every week, as she stands firm on government control of our lives. Even though there is majority taxpayer opposition to her position, she will not yield. What makes her destructive politics worse is that we the people can't unelect her unless we live in her district in California. She comes from a small socialist district in San Francisco and only her constituents can unselect her. Its not right that she can control our lives, but we can not decide to have her kicked out of congress. She must be removed from the majority and put back in the minority, or voted out of office as soon as possible. Everyone should understand; it is Pelosi who lives like royalty on taxpayer dollars and behaves like a queen. Pelosi thinks she is the Princess Diana of America. She treats people like her servants and she splurges fax dollars without any care for our future.

□□

Speaker Pelosi often requests military aircraft to fly her, her family, and her colleagues around the country. Representatives for judicial watch obtained emails and other important documents from a Freedom of Information request stating that these documents clearly show Pelosi's abuse of her powers by splurging taxpayer dollars. She has treated the Air force as her "personal air fleet." Naturally, her office claimed that these were lies and pointed to White House Policy enacted after September 11, 2001, which allows the Speaker to travel to her district via military aircraft. Her staff claims that she uses the same type of military aircraft that was used by her predecessor, Dennis Hastert. Upon further investigations, it was uncovered that she repeatedly made special demands for high-end aircraft and last minute cancellations. This irresponsible behavior cost hundreds of thousands of dollars in expenses for taxpayers! Some of her emails showed she was arrogant and demanding because of her high position of power. She used the Department of Defense officials as her servants and demanded accommodations, which were outside of the norm. One researcher in the group stated, "I think that's above and beyond what other members of Congress are doing and what is expected of our elected officials." Her aids complained in an email that the military did not make available any aircraft the House Speaker wanted for Memorial Day recess. In her email, Pelosi's staff wrote, "It is my understanding there are NO G5s available for the House during the Memorial Day recess. This is totally unacceptable ... The Speaker will want to know where the planes are." When a certain type of aircraft was not available, her staffer wrote, "This is not good news, and we will have some very disappointed folks, as well as a very upset Speaker."

Pelosi disrespects everyone from taxpayers to brave military personnel. This woman belongs in prison for abuse of power! The arrogance of the Speaker is beyond comprehension; she is lying, misleading, and acting like an authoritarian dictator.

To show how little she cares for any of us Americans, we need to look at the stimulus package. Nancy Pelosi showed more concern for a desert rat in California than American taxpayers who were losing their homes, jobs, retirement accounts, and just about anything else they worked hard for. The stimulus plan of 2009 included a $30 million bailout for wetlands restorations to spend in San Francisco Bay Areas to protect a desert RAT! Pelosi represents the City of San Francisco and has previously shown concern for the RAT. Only Democrats would put RATS ahead of taxpayers.

☐☐

Pelosi also accused the CIA of misleading congress. The CIA is the secret spy organization, which employs brave, unnamed American service men who put their lives in danger on foreign soil every day. The CIA agents are the people who, when caught in dangerous places around the world, are actually tortured for real. This is not Guantanamo Bay torture; this is real torture pulling out fingernails, breaking bones and beating within inches of their lives, electric shocks, and more. They are the real spies, the Special Forces, the Jack Bowers and GI Joes of the world who keep America safe from terrorists and rogue nations. These are the very people Nancy Pelosi accused of lying. What she did is considered TREASON! SHE DOES NOT CARE ABOUT YOU! SHE CARES ABOUT TOTAL POWER! Just imagine the woman who cares more about a desert rat and goes out of her way to send money to restore wetlands turns around and blatantly accuses brave Americans in the CIA of lying to her. Pelosi is so arrogant that when questioned about the CIA, Pelosi told the press, "I'm not answering questions about the CIA anymore." HOW DARE SHE! She accuses the CIA of treason! Yes, TREASON. She boldly stated that the CIA mislead and lied to Congress. That would mean the CIA is committing treason against the U.S.A. When the press asked her about it, she said, "NO MORE QUESTIONS ON THAT SUBJECT!" What happened to our media? I thought they were supposed to be looking out for us. Pelosi disrespected an agency in which thousands of brave Americans put their lives in harm's way, risking their lives for our safety. A woman in such a high place of power should not be allowed to tell lies about our brave men and women who risk their lives for this country. Where is our media? Why are they not demanding for her to step down?□

□

This is the same woman who, when chosen to be Speaker of the House, stated that she would clean up Washington. She is the same woman who thought that changing the House lunch menu was more important than affordable energy for the hardworking American people. Instead of removing government control from our lives, she decided to put more flowers in the Capitol Building. While you were packing your bags and moving out of your house, Pelosi was picking out her travel plans around the world. The Speaker of the House was vacationing in the Middle East with terrorists while you were getting your late credit card notices from your bank! Nancy Pelosi was busy flying around in military aircraft while your bank was calling you to foreclose on your home. The Speaker of the

House of the United States was more concerned about getting Obama elected and destroying our economy, hence our lives. She broke the public trust by manipulating the economy to suit her needs instead of ensuring a healthy environment for us to be able to stay employed and keep our homes.

☐   When government stands by and purposely interrupts the flow of commerce and business in our economy, it is a form of attacking its own people from within. The federal departments are no different from a group of terrorist organizations terrorizing freedom-loving Americans. When gasoline prices go up, so does the price of everything else we buy, and this restricts our freedoms. This takes money out of our pockets and forces us to spend more on basic needs: food, fuel, and shelter. The big trucks, which deliver goods to the stores, must charge more for delivery when the price of fuel goes up. Some of these big trucks spend thousands of dollars on fuel each month just to deliver the goods to the supermarkets. This in turn gets carried over to you and I, the consumer, and we end up paying for it through higher food prices. This is what Nancy Pelosi and the Democrats gave us. The federal government's hunger for power has created a recession, which is sinking us deeper into debt.

☐

Congress uses their power to manipulate our lives and make us behave in certain ways. Sadly, most Americans do not bother to look into this. Ignorant media and voters allow Nancy Pelosi to get away with blaming Big Oil, Big Banks, and Big Insurance companies anyone but the real people responsible for the damages done. Pelosi is the one in charge; she can free us from the shackles of this tyrannical federal government. She instead used her powers to increase the size of the federal government and crush the private sector! She answers to no one. Pelosi lies and blames insurance companies for the high cost of healthcare, when the truth is the real corruption is in the government-run Medicare (to the tune of over $40 billion in 2008 alone). People who follow Health Care issues know the real people responsible for high costs are tort lawyers and government departments issuing mandates.

□□

In 2009, Our nation is under the rule of the Democratic Party. It is clear that Pelosi and the democrats are attempting to turn the U.S.A. into the U.S.S.A. United Socialist States of America. Once we reach that point, the way out will be dangerous and possibly violent. History has shown us that socialist nations always crumble within. If the Democratic Party and their leadership do not alter the direction in which they are taking us, they will have to answer to the American taxpayer. Thoughts of The Magna-Carta come to mind.□Nancy Pelosi must be stripped of her powers and removed from the position as Speaker of the House; she is the root of all-evil in our government today. We should all do our civic duty and contact our representative via email, telephone, or snail mail demanding that Pelosi be removed from the position of Speaker!

□□

-- Send Washington a message: "IMPEACH PELOSI!"--

com-mun-ism (kom-yuh-niz-uhm), n.

1. a theory or system of social organization based on the holding of all property in common, actual ownership being ascribed to the community as a whole or to the state

2. a system of social organization in which all economic and social activity is controlled by a totalitarian state dominated by a single and self-perpetuating political party

Who is Barack Hussein Obama? Just about everyone in the U.S.A., or, for that matter, in the world, knows this. Or do they? One obvious answer is that he is the 44th president of the United States of America, or the first affirmative action President. But does the average American voter actually know his opinions or his ideology? Do people understand his ideas and beliefs? Do people actually understand his vision for our country and the world?□ □ □

Her are just a few:

Government-controlled healthcare

Higher taxes for all Americans

More environmental policies and taxes for energy usage

Government-controlled banks and corporations

Distributing people' s wealth

Plainly put, turning America into a socialist country like the old Soviet Union once was. If you were to ask the average American, or, for that matter, the average Washington insider, to name something important that Barack Obama has accomplished while in the United States Senate or the Illinois State Senate, they would not be able to name ONE, not ONE! That is because he has no accomplishments. Obama was a community organizer...whatever that means. Just what is a community organizer? Nobody knows for certain. If we look back at history and try to name some famous community organizers, the only name that pops into my head is the honorable Reverend Al Sharpton. He is a famous community organizer, just not as successful as Obama. Also, he is not as clean and articulate as Barack Obama. That's probably why the Reverend Sharpton has such a hard time appealing to the American voter. Other than organizing the community, Barack Obama has not accomplished anything. He never had to prove himself, thanks to affirmative action. Affirmative action is a law that promotes people because of the color of their skin and not because of their accomplishments or qualifications. Let's face it; if people looked at Obama's resume, and listened to him explain complex issues face to face, one would think there are two different people. One which looks great on resume and one in real life which sounds great while reading a tele-prompter. What is a community organizer any way? Is it someone who goes around the community and promises people government for handouts? No one is really sure. After he community organized and registered thousands of voters, Obama trained more community organizers to take his place while he focused his skills on running for the Illinois State Senate in 1996. He was a skillful politician who manipulated his way to win a seat in the Illinois Senate. He did this by effectively using election rules to have the incumbent Democratic competitors disqualified! He invalidated the voting petition of three of the candidates there by running unchallenged and unopposed. He was the only one on the ballot!

While in the Illinois State Senate, he accomplished absolutely NOTHING! Obama never wrote a bill; he only sponsored bills and voted up, down, or present on all bills that came up. He was absent of leadership. When a juvenile crime bill came up for vote, Obama did not vote for or against the bill. In fact, he voted present on bills over 120 times! The juvenile crime bill would have treated some extremely violent juveniles as adults and saved innocent lives from violent gangbangers. This risked his good standing with the African-Americans; therefore, he decided to be neither for nor against the bill.

He is not experienced; he does not understand civics or the free market economy. He is skilled as a politician with slick marketing, campaigning, and the support of corrupt organizations like ACORN and the Black Panthers. After eight years of wasting taxpayer money and watching Illinois and Chicago deteriorate from the Illinois State Senate, Obama saw an even greater opportunity present itself the chance to run for the U.S. Senate. At that time, he was running against a formidable Republican candidate named Jack Ryan. As usual, Barack Obama was out of his league. With no legislative experience and no laws he could put his name to, he was the empty suit running with nothing but his charm and his skills as a politician capable of mastering the teleprompter. Obama decided to put his political skills to the test and have this opponent, Jack Ryan, disqualified just like when he ran for Illinois Senate. Once he had Jack Ryan disqualified with the aid of the media, Barack Obama won a seat in the U.S. Senate. Dr. Alan Keys, a well-respected conservative black American and a man who is passionate about his beliefs, ran against Obama. With just a couple of months to prepare a campaign, there was not much for time Dr. Alan Keyes to get his campaign in gear and his message out, it was too late to pose a meaningful challenge to Obama.

□□

Obama was elevated to the level he is at because of his charisma, socialist ideology, and his teleprompter skills. He became famous when he gave a speech at the Democratic convention in 2004, ever since then, he has mesmerized the Democratic Party. His backers also chose him, as he mastered the art of giving speeches and reading the teleprompter. He had his ignorant voter base and the corrupt Illinois political system to thank for winning a seat in the U.S. Senate. When the opportunity came to run for president, Obama threw his hat in the race and decided to run. Once he came out as the clear choice by the Democratic Party, he had to prepare to face John McCain, who was representing the Republicans. Obama's backers knew that he would not perform well in a head-to-head debate against McCain, so they decided to keep him away from debates until the very last minute. During the presidential campaign, McCain challenged Obama to over 20 debates. Obama rejected McCain's offer and suggested that they have one debate on the July 4, 2008. Obviously, the Obama team knew that not many Americans would watch a presidential debate during the holidays. This is the kind of manipulation and deception he used to win the White House. The Obama puppet masters knew that the way to keep Obama popular was to have him keep giving speeches, which he read off tele-prompters every step of the way.

We should not forget that a people who are in a position of power because of affirmative action, don't know how to manage their newfound powers; they know what they read off sheets and tele-prompters. His performance as an Illinois State Senator tells us all we need to know about his qualifications. He has never written any laws. In fact, Barack Obama has consistently been on the WRONG side of the law. In Illinois, he did not support a bill to prosecute violent juveniles as adults. He favored late term abortion bills that seemed unethical. In the long run, not passing these kinds of bills has had a devastating impact to the Illinois communities. In Chicago, the 2008 murder rate was up 18% compared to the first seven months of 2007. This is Obama's territory. He, as a Senator, was directly responsible for passing laws to curb the rise in crime. Looking back, perhaps supporting and demanding prosecution of violent juveniles could have helped reduce crime rates. Thousands of innocent Chicago residents are suffering because of Obama's lack of leadership and arrogance. Now that Obama has been elevated to new heights, we are seeing millions of Americans feel the destructive decisions of Barack Obama! This is all due to ignorance of the elites and the uneducated who do not take the time to learn the truth about the people who are deciding their faith and their destiny.

Obama's position as Illinois Senator has been devastating for Illinois state residents. Since Obama left the Chicago Senate, the crime rate has been on the rise, unemployment has gone up, and corruption has reached levels Chicago has not seen before. How can he possibly help solve any problems in this country? He hasn't done a thing to make his own state a better place for the residents. Obama's solutions are all socialist solutions, which will damage this country and hurt millions of citizens. He believes in socialism and equality in the eyes of the federal government. He believes the government is the answer, and he will work as hard as he can to ensure government is involved in every part of our lives. Most of you may ask, "What is wrong with being equal? Everyone should be equal." Can anyone really say what being equal is? Does it mean we all have the same house, same car, same washer, dryer, and refrigerator? Does it mean we all make the same amount and we all have Blackberry telephones? That would mean no one has anything better than his or her neighbor. Is that really the kind of world we want to live in? That lifestyle was tried in communist countries. The simple fact is if everyone were equal and the same, then there would be no reason to live because there is nothing exciting or interesting to look forward to. If we are all going to be equal, then why have the Olympics? Why play any sports? We are all equal anyway, so no one is going to win. Every football game would end at 7-7, every baseball game would tie at 2-2, and so on. Equality is a socialist word that promises utopia. In fact, it is the worst kind of hell we can be subjected to. The only thing that should be equal is the way our laws treats all citizens and politicians alike.

Do we want to live in Obama country? In Obama country, one central government controls everything in our lives. They control banks, corporations, the medical industry, education, and social security! How far do we want to let government go? Obama wants to control all that and more. By the time his four years in the White House are over, he will attempt to take over every aspect of our lives and dictate how much we can earn. With Nancy Pelosi and Harry Reid on Obama's side, they will have the federal government in charge of anything and everything. Who are the people programming Obama's teleprompter? We don't really know; it could be David Axelrod or Rom Emanuel. Some suspect its George Soros. The real Obama is your average socialist who doesn't know anything other than what he learned from communist mentors, racist preachers and elitist socialist professors in Ivy League Schools. Some people think Obama knows, but he actually reads off a teleprompter. It's sad, but it is true. In his press interviews, all his questions are preselected, and the answers are written for him on the teleprompter. Obama depends on the teleprompter so much that he even needed it to announce a cabinet member and give a speech to a group of 6th graders

☐

To get an idea of how clueless Obama is without a tele-prompter, we can look at the first public signing ceremony of a bill to close Guantanamo prison in Cuba the prison where dangerous terrorists are imprisoned. A lawyer named Gregory B. Craig placed a bill in front of Obama to sign. Unfortunately Obama had no clue about what was in the bill. After the signing of the bill, the press started asking questions about the bill, Obama had a clueless look on his face and turned to his lawyer, Gregory Craig, to ask him the same questions a reporter just asked him. Finally, Gregory Craig answered the press in detail about the questions that were originally posed to President Obama, the person who signed the bill. Obama did the same thing that our Congress is doing with the stimulus bill, the cap and trade bill, the cash for clunkers deal, and our healthcare bill. He did not know what it contained, nor did he bother to read it. He just signed it! All he knew was that it had something to do with closing Guantanamo Bay Prison, a prison, which houses the most dangerous terrorists in the world. ☐With no teleprompter to read off, Obama was lost. In other words, he didn't know the answer to any of the questions about the bill he just signed! President Obama is a direct result of affirmative action. He mastered the art of tele-prompter reading, and he impressed elitist socialists in a speech at the Democratic Convention in 2004 when John Kerry ran against George Bush. George Soros, Nancy Pelosi, and most of the U.S. mainstream media were so impressed that they put their support behind Obama because they were impressed by his speech. Pelosi backed him because she saw someone who would not oppose her, someone she could mold like clay in her hands. With Obama in the White House, Pelosi saw the opportunity to pass just about every socialist agenda Democrats have dreamed of for the past 20 years. Barack Obama is sitting in the oval office waiting for something to sign. This man truly does not know what is going on. He is only able to comment on things that are on his teleprompter. Anyone can find an Obama speech on you tube to hear and see him as he gives his pre written answers to pre-screened questions from the press.

☐

Pre-screened questions? Teleprompter answers? What kind of person is running our country? Who is running our country? It sounds like Nancy Pelosi and whoever is writing the words on the teleprompter are actually running our country. This is what happens when people stop paying attention to the real world and get absorbed into the superficial world of celebrity news and junk entertainment. It is November 2009, and unemployment just hit 9.5% and is estimated to keep rising. The future looks dark and uncertain. We need change, but this is not the change we need. We need less government and more competent leaders, ones who do not need a teleprompter to answer questions or do just about anything regarding matters of national security.

☐☐

Its hard to believe that in the short year since Barack Obama was elected president, our jobless rate jumped 100%, the federal deficit went up over $1 trillion dollars in the first six months, the financial system has been wrecked and taken over by the mob in the federal government, the auto companies ended up going on government welfare, and we are about to lose our rights to affordable healthcare. While the taxpayers are going broke and losing everything, President Obama takes his wife out to dinner in New York and gets pizza deliveries from Chicago! He throws rock concerts at the White House, plays basketball and golf, and has shady questionable communist visitors in the White House. He consistently ignores the, real problems of the world. He ignores Africa, (Bush went to Africa and gave $50 million to help fight and cure Aids). Obama has roots in Africa, yet he has not visited or even brought his family to visit. Every American born in the U.S. has been fortunate to be born here instead of anywhere else in the world! Obama doesn't know this or appreciate this; it is why he wants to change America. If Obama gets his way, being born in America will be no different from being born anywhere else in the world. The worst part about it is, there will be nowhere left to escape to for freedom-loving people.

If Obama were for positive change, his message would have been to get the federal government out of our lives starting with the Department of Energy, OSHA, education, the IRS, the Department of Commerce, the United States Postal Service, and every other government-run agency. Privatize the post office and we will see profits instead of deficits! Close federal departments and unemployment will drop to 4% or less. We must encourage the government to close every department they have created in the past 100 years for the sake of saving the United States from bankruptcy. Obama doesn't think about these things because he doesn't understand how our economy works! This is exactly why the federal government must yield its power back to the citizens of the United States. We can't jeopardize the lives of over 300 million Americans to the hands of an affirmative action president.

The third most powerful person is the Senate Majority Leader, Harry Reid. Another typical Democrat politician who manipulated his way to power, Harry Reid has made millions since being in the Senate. When he became a powerful Senator, he traded favors for land gifts and used his powers to enrich himself.

In 2002, Harry Reid (D-Nev.) paid $10,000 to a pension fund controlled by his long-time friend and lubricant distributor, Claire Haycock. The payment gave Senator Reid total control of 160-acres of land in Bullhead City that Senator Reid and the pension fund had jointly owned. Senator Reid's buy-in price of $10,000 was estimated to be the equivalent of buying six acres of land. Six months after the land deal closed, Senator Reid introduced legislation to address the hardship of lubricant dealers who had their supplies disrupted by oil companies. The land deal was clearly a payoff for Reid's political clout. Just so everyone is aware, the mainstream media does not investigate corrupt Democrats unless it is impossible to cover up their crimes. This was not worth investigating because people didn't really know who Harry Reid was, so he had no worries. When the crime is exposed and it happens to be a Democrat, MSNBC, NBC, ABC, and CBS will not mention it. If they have no choice, they go out of their way to make excuses for the Democrats. You don't hear them talk about Harry Reid, or Charlie Rangel, or John Conyers, or Chuck Schumer. All these politicians have committed unethical and criminal acts that should have impeached them from their positions of power. When the press questioned Senate Minority Leader Harry Reid's windfall land deal, Harry Reid hung up the phone! Senate Minority Leader Harry Reid denied any wrongdoing when he collected a $1.1 million windfall profit on a Las Vegas land sale. When the property deeds were examined, its showed Senator Reid hadn't personally owned the property for three years. When asked, Reid says he hasn't done anything wrong. If the Senate Ethics Committee orders him to, he is willing to change his report on the transaction.

□□

That was the end of the query into Senator Reid's extremely profitable land deals. Democrats like Obama, Reid, and Pelosi are allowed to tell the press to go stuff it, and the press obeys. Republicans try that, and they are crucified and end up resigning within a short period of time. Harry Reid is not looking out for the hardworking taxpayer. Harry Reid and his Democratic allies are disrespecting all American workers from all walks of life blue-collar to white-collar workers. As the leader of the Democrats in the Senate, Reid's whole motivation while in the minority was to get the majority back in the Senate and make Bush look like public enemy number one. Being the Senate Minority Leader and then later the Majority Leader, Harry Reid has as much responsibility as Nancy Pelosi when it comes to ensuring that our nation is safe and people's rights are protected. Unfortunately, Reid's whole motivation during his term was not about keeping us safe; it was about self-enrichment and making President George Bush look bad. Some of his tactics included badmouthing the president in front of a group of high school kids.

In 2005, in Las Vegas, Nevada, while speaking to students in an American Studies class at Del Sol High School, Senator Reid spoke of President George W. Bush and said, "I think this guy is a loser." Later on, Reid was asked if his comment about Bush would create problems in negotiations with Republicans. He replied, "I tell people how I feel about things. I don't try to hide how I feel," Reid said. *"Maybe my choice of words was improper, and I have indicated that maybe they were, but I want everyone here, I repeat, to know I'm going to continue to call things the way that I see them, and I think this administration has done a very, very bad job for this nation and the world."* Later on, Reid acknowledged his comment was wrong, and he called White House advisor Karl Rove to apologize.

Harry Reid has no respect for President Bush and the Bush doctrine against terrorists. If someone does not understand the Bush doctrine, I will explain it now: KEEP AMERICA SAFE FROM TERRORIST ATTACKS. Unfortunately, our elitist politicians and the talking heads on television don't seem to get it. When Harry Reid came out and called President Bush a loser in front of a group of high school students, that showed how little respect he had for George bush and how little he cared about the safety and security of the American people. To make matters worse, Harry Reid publicly announced that the War in Iraq was lost! It seems his Democratic allies did not stand by his side when he made this insulting comment.

□□

It does not end there with Senator Reid. After he finished insulting and badmouthing our president, Senator Reid decided to attack our energy companies, specifically coal. Without any care or hesitation, he singled out and ridiculed the very industries that are responsible for affordable energy all across America. Instead, Harry Reid blames these companies for creating man made global warming, which is a complete hoax and a myth. According to Harry Reid man and energy companies are responsible for global warming.

. □□

In September 2008, according to U.S. Senator Jim DeMint's blog posted, even though House Democrats were considering lifting the extending bans on offshore drilling and oil shale in the continuing resolution (CR) appropriations bill, Democrat Senate Leader Harry Reid decided to sneak an extension of the oil shale ban through as Congress fought over the financial bailout. Oil shale in America's west is estimated to hold between 800 billion and 2 trillion barrels of oil that is more than the proven oil reserves in Saudi Arabia alone.

□

Just like before, Harry Reid is still playing politics with our lives when we need help the most. With unemployment over 10%, our leaders are taking all the wrong steps to bring jobs and prosperity back. Instead of cutting taxes and regulations on the private sector, Pelosi, Reid, and Obama are advocating more federal intervention, regulation and bailouts for banks.

The problem with Harry Reid's beliefs about global warming is that they are not proven. In fact, there has not been one concrete piece of evidence that Man has anything to do whatsoever with the global temperatures. Unfortunately, because Harry Reid believes otherwise, we, the taxpayers, are punished by having to pay more taxes for our energy usage. Here in the United States, we have more energy than in the Middle East. Harry Reid does not care about our own oil reserves; he makes his decisions based on a myth that man is causing global warming. Harry Reid is one of the three most powerful people in our nation, and he is steering our nation in a direction which is hurting innocent Americans. Reid, like Pelosi, is responsible for the price of oil rising and unemployment doubling in the past year. In September of 2008, when the economy was falling, lawmakers were panicking and not sure what to do. Even Senate Leader Harry Reid came out and said, *"No one knows what to do,"* that day Harry Reid told us that our elected leaders are not capable of fixing the financial meltdown they created. This crisis was caused by high price of energy and years of neglecting FANNIE MAE and FREDDIE MAC, the center point of our recent financial meltdown! It is the responsibility of Congress and the Senate to oversee we have adequate supplies of energy and that FannieMae and FreddieMac are operated responsibly. These are the agencies Harry Reid did not deem necessary to investigate and fix!

☐☐

The three people mentioned in this chapter are the most

powerful people in the world in 2009. Their decisions and their hunger for power and control over our everyday lives are costing us billions of dollars every month from Obama's plans to have government control everything to Nancy Pelosi's vision of government-controlled healthcare to Harry Reid's vision of America without coal or oil. These people have an ideology that is very different from that which built this great nation. The current leaders of these institutions are all national socialists. Their goal is to create a government that decides everything, from what we drive, what our home loan will be, what our social security retirement will be, and the kind of light bulbs we must use, to what version of history our children learn in schools. This government will decide your healthcare from cradle to the grave. They will not stop seeking power over our lives. If we look back 50 years, we will see that we have been steadily losing our freedoms through the creation of new federal departments. Congress has been creating new ways to have more power and control over our lives. The ones in powerful positions the Speaker, the President, the Majority Leader are all conspiring to become even more powerful and to gain even more control over our lives.

☐

Congress has a huge problem with money. They are addicted to spending it. Just look at whom they selected as their leaders. Pelosi and Reid are the biggest spenders out there! The projected deficit for 2009 is currently estimated at $1.9 trillion! The people in Congress have absolutely no concern of the damages they are inflicting on the American people's wealth and way of life. They have not a care in the world of how much money they print, how much inflation they create, and how far in debt they put us. The White House projected 2009 deficit will reach $1.75 trillion. The projections for 2010 will also be larger than projected, totaling $1.4 trillion. In its budget request to Congress, the administration said that 2010 deficit would total $1.17 trillion.☐☐ What makes this even more dangerous is that government has the power to print all the money they want. Why would they stop? No one is stopping them. The media does not question their spending or their printing of money, reporters are no longer doing the job that the American people expect of them. The mainstream media has an agenda in par with the Democratic leadership and that is why we do not see any changes in our government.

Unless we, the people, change who are leaders are on election day, we will get another layer of bureaucrats complicating every existing federal program and our lives. We must take powers away from the federal government! The American people must unite on closing all federal departments or our future will be doomed! If we can get government to close departments one by one, it would slowly take way the power and control from our elected leaders the power they have been using to abuse us, destroy lives, and practice their insane socialist ideologies. Congress is so misguided that they believe putting mercury-filled toxic light bulbs in our homes will save the planet. The people in Congress are dangerous, and they shouldn't be allowed to continue destroying our lives.

☐☐

The three people discussed in this chapter have done tremendous damage to our lives. Pelosi alone controls more of our lives than we realize. One person in a group of 432 representatives decides what we pay for gasoline, or what the minimum wage should be for millions of people, or the environmental laws we must live by. This one person knows nothing about how much expensive energy and high taxes hurt people! There are so many federal taxes and fees that most of us couldn't even calculate how much taxes we really pay. Income taxes, business taxes, medial taxes, and social security taxes and hundreds of other taxes we don't see because manufacturers pass them on to us when we buy their products. We are busy living our lives, and not many of us have time to catch up on what goes on in Washington, D.C. every day. We have our own lives to live, but now it's come to a point where we have to pay attention or it will be the end of our way of life, the way of American life.

The best government department is a government department in charge of closing down government departments. Visit www.destructivepolitics.com send an email to Congress, tell them to close these departments starting with the Department of Energy and give us back our freedoms!

Committee on Agriculture

Committee on Appropriations

Committee on Armed Services

Committee on the Budget

Committee on Education and Labor

Committee on Energy and Commerce

Committee on Financial Services

Committee on Foreign Affairs

Committee on Homeland Security

Committee on House Administration

Committee on the Judiciary

Committee on Natural Resources

Committee on Oversight and Government Reform

Committee on Rules

Committee on Science and Technology

Committee on Small Business

Committee on Standards of Official Conduct

Committee on Transportation and Infrastructure

Committee on Veterans' Affairs

Committee on Ways and Means

Joint Economic Committee

Joint Congressional Committee on Inaugural Ceremonies

Joint Committee on Taxation

House Permanent Select Committee on Intelligence

House Select Committee on Energy Independence and Global Warming

===================
Chapter 2 – Global Warming
===================

"If we are truly destroying the planet, then why is the planet not destroying us?"

O ur environment is complex, as is evident by the variety of differing views from the scientific community. From the year-round summer in the tropics to the never-ending winter in the north and south poles, earth's climate varies by as much as 80 degrees Fahrenheit or more on a daily basis. Earth has been around for 4.5 billion years with all kinds of changing weather conditions, from burning hot to ice cold. Currently, we are fortunate to be living during a period of relatively low volcanic activity and earthquakes. At this time, the climate of this planet suits our living conditions. Weather on earth is affected by everything from sunspot cycles, objects in space, the gravitational effects of our moon and planets, and ocean currents to volcanic activity and other major natural events. The complex influence and interaction of all of these factors are the primary drivers that determine our climate. The insignificant effect of human activity and industrialization has absolutely no effect on global climate.

☐

Even though there is no proof that human activity has had any significant or catastrophic effect on our global climate, there are groups of environmentalists who claim that humankind is directly responsible for destroying our planet. The problem with our global environmental movement is that the people who claim to speak for the environment are misleading the public to further their agenda. In November 2009, it was reported that scientists in the University of East Anglia's Climatic Research Unit had purposely misled the world about climate change. They held back data and manipulated the news around which environmental laws were created. Other organizations such as Green Peace, Earth Liberation Front (ELF), Earth First, The United Nations and other extreme environmental organizations are using the global environment as a way to get the unsuspecting public to agree with junk science and pay higher fees. These organizations and groups guilt us into believing that we are destroying this planet just because of the way we live. This is an absurd effort orchestrated by these groups to convince the public to buy into their propaganda. We are NOT destroying this planet; we will live on this planet until the time comes when the earth decides that we are no longer fit to occupy it. This will happen in the very distant future, and it will be determined by the course of naturally occurring events, which are likely beyond human control. Earth's climate has undergone significant changes over the past 4.5 billion of years all driven by natural events, not humans.

□□

Within the relatively short span of human existence, we have seen planet earth flex its massive natural forces of destruction. One that comes to mind in recent times is the eruption of Mount Saint Helens in May 1980. The eruption of Mount Saint Helens emitted a significant amount of volcanic ash and gases, such as sulfur dioxide and carbon dioxide, into the atmosphere. The eruption, which took the lives of 56 people, also damaged or destroyed over 4 billion board feet (14.6 km³) of timber, killed an estimated 6,500 deer and elk, and wiped out an estimated 15 million Chinook and Coho salmon and millions of birds and small mammals. Over 200 square miles of thick, rich forest disappeared in a single day. Just 25 years later, in December 2004, we witnessed a giant Tsunami in the Indian Ocean, which claimed the lives of over 250,000 humans and reshaped the coastlines of some Asian countries. This is proof that Mother Nature is not concerned about us. If we are to survive, we must learn to adapt to the turbulent changes our planet undergoes. The turbulent changes in nature have existed ever since the earth was formed over 4.5billion years ago.

Unfortunately, people are falling for the propaganda that human behavior is changing the global climate and causing these natural disasters. There is no proof that human activity has anything to do with the global climate or any natural disasters. Regardless of these facts, false information is spread daily by our government, media, and socialist organizations pretending to be guardians of the environment. They manipulate data and trick taxpayers into contributing money and paying higher taxes because they claim our way of life is polluting the planet. This is wrong and extremely misguided. The effects of human industrial and non-industrial activity have been proven to have absolutely NO affect on the global temperature. The truth is one violent volcanic eruption can devastate local environments as evident by MT Saint Helen in 1980 or MT Pinatubo in the Philippines in 1991, mother nature always cleans it up in due time.

Our government's fight for a clean environment is no longer about a clean environment. It has become a quest to control our energy use and our rate of consumption here in America. Under the cloak of environmentalists, socialists hijacked our federal government and created new regulations and taxes to control the way we live. These controlling authorities cost us taxpayers billions of dollars in unnecessary fees and lost jobs every year. On top of it, they serve no benefit to the environment. By mandating fuels like ethanol made from corn to our gasoline, the Federal Energy Department is actually hurting the environment and poor people around the world. Through controlling authorities, or as they call them, departments, our leaders in Washington, D.C. are punishing us for causing global warming and pollution! Meanwhile, politicians receive kickbacks and favors for forcing taxpayers to use ethanol as a clean fuel additive to gasoline.

Voices of reason and truth, which try to convince people that we are not causing global warming, are drowned out by the powers that be in Congress and the media. Instead, People like former Vice President Al Gore give speeches warning us of global warming in the middle of blizzards. Our government has corrupted the mainstream media so much so that reporters no longer question global climate change. These media elites are so gullible that if they see ice melt, they rush over with a film crew to report ice melting, and then they blame it on corporations. With all the evidence proving global climate change is not caused by man, our media and government will not back down. Congress has conspired and joined forces with environmentalists to promote, tax, and mislead our population. On top of that, they give environmentalists grants to further their environmentalist agenda. People fell for these lies and still believe the government will do the right thing and save the environment no matter what it takes. The punishments we endure from our federal government restrict our freedoms, and create high unemployment, which hurts the poor and the middle class the most. The poor rely on affordable energy the most, yet they are the ones most hurt by Pelosi and Obama's energy policy. Obama, Pelosi, and Reid put their trust into expensive bio-fuels, which caused the price of food and gasoline to rise. Under Reid and Pelosi's leadership, congress chooses to ignore people falling on hard times and losing jobs and eventually homes. While America is falling deeper into recession, democrats create more obstacles for job creation by ensuring energy stays expensive along with higher taxes and more complex regulations.

☐

Instead of finding out the truth about the global climate and bio fuels, Obama, Pelosi, and Reid are preoccupied with how to ration our energy and control our carbon output. They ignore REAL facts about global carbon output and tell us that what we know is wrong. Under the guise of lies, our government is charging ahead, destroying our economy and taking away much needed affordable energy. Congress completely ignores accurate temperature readings of the past 100 years, which prove that the earth has in fact been cooling! Yes, it has been cooling since the late 1990s, according to weather data collected by multiple sources around the world. "What about the ice melting?" you may ask. Ice has been forming and melting for billions of years. Its ice; it will melt! ☐

☐

Regardless of the undeniable fact that human behavior has no effect on global climate or increased carbon emissions in the environment, vice president Al Gore and Congress don't care! Most Americans have no idea that the House of Representatives passed the cap and trade energy tax bill in June 2009. The Democrats secured the vote of one Ohioan, Democratic Rep. Marcy Kaptur of Toledo. The Democrats got her vote the old-fashioned way. They gave her everything she wanted, and they sold out our futures by rewarding Rep. Kaptur with a new federal power authority, similar to Washington State's Bonneville Power Administration. It is ready to go with over $3.5 billion in taxpayer money available for lending to renewable energy and economic development projects in Ohio and other Mid-Western states. In the winter of 2009-2010, the U.S. Senate is preparing to pass this cap and trade energy bill, if this bill becomes law, it will more than triple the cost of our electricity! It will also increase the price of gasoline along with everything else we buy. Here are some facts about what the cap and trade bill will do to us if the Senate passes it: ☐

1. *Make it more expensive for you to heat your home in the cold winter*
2. *Increase the price of the gasoline you buy when you drive to work*
3. *Increase the price of food (because the cost of fuel will be higher for people delivering food and costs will be passed along to consumers)*
4. *Make the electricity we depend on more expensive*
5. *Make businesses pay higher energy tax, which will also be passed on to consumers*

We will also see more people lose their jobs and many poor and elderly freeze to death thanks to the cap and trade bill.

The government says we need cap and trade because we are emitting too much pollution into the atmosphere and ice is melting! Our leaders in Congress are accepting the myth that the polar icecaps are melting because of the American way of life. Imagine that! There are six billion people in the world, but just 300 million living in America are causing the ice to melt! But wait a minute… Wasn't there an ice age a few thousand years ago? About 10 thousand years ago, there was so much ice on earth that snow covered most of the North American continent down to the middle of the United States. How will we know when that ice age will be over? How do we know how much ice there was in the North Pole when the ice age began? With all this ice melting, archeologists are discovering frozen remains of prehistoric people, vegetation, tropical plants, and animals. Could it be that the area now covered with giant icebergs was once free of ice and snow? I'm no scientist, but I would imagine that perhaps, at one time, before humans came along or maybe during human activity, there was a tropical forest with all kinds of animals thriving on land now covered by icebergs. The truth is human made global warming does NOT exist. If someone tells you that we are affecting the temperature of the planet, ask him or her what the correct temperature is. How do we know the planet is getting warmer if we don't know what the "right" temperature is?

□□

America prospered over the past 200 years because we had all the affordable energy we needed and we didn't kill the planet using all that energy. We created a powerful nation by using the oil Mother Nature provided to us while protecting and nurturing our environment. We spread prosperity around the world, thereby improving lives of billions of people and their environments. Somewhere along the way, environmentalists took control of our government and turned our government against us in the name of global warming. For the past 100 years, governments have been creating a wedge between the voters and our elected officials by regulating our consumption. One of the most destructive departments to regulate our lives was created on August 4, 1977. The federal government created the Department of Energy to control our nation's energy consumption. Today, Nancy Pelosi uses the department of energy to crush our lives and weaken our economy. She deliberately holds back much needed energy from all of us by making it more expensive in the name of global warming. Department of energy chairman Henry Waxman, with Pelosi's full support, is working on passing cap and trade which will cost more American jobs than we lost in 2008-2009—all in the name of global warming. Facts and reality show us that there is nothing wrong with the global environment. The lies these people have been telling us compounded so much in the past 40 years that many believe our behavior is truly causing the planet to warm!

□□

Our planet is NOT warming because of us, and it is certainly not dying! The reality is, we can only damage the environment around us. If we all start to throw our trash in the streets and pollute our rivers and lakes, we will harm our immediate environment and create a health hazard. This happens in poor nations around the world. In the U.S with the exception of government-run projects, our towns and cities are clean cleaner than the average street in South America, Europe, Asia, or Africa. Yet, it is America that is getting punished for polluting the planet. Here are some real FACTS about planet earth. These following truths are undeniable!

1.   The earth is 4,523,499,435 years old, give or take a few hundred million years
2. The earth has gone through hundreds of ice ages, in which this planet was literally a giant ball of snow and ice.
3. The Island of Manhattan NYC was covered by one-mile ice sheet about 10,000 years ago!
4. American Indians wandered across the north pole from Europe thousands of years ago when a giant sheet of ice connected Europe and North America.
5.   Gigantic volcanic eruptions can create significant amount of pollution, which can cause short-term changes to otherwise normal temperatures.
6.   The temperature of the earth varies; the sun provides heat and life for our planet.
7. Mother Nature is in control of global climate.
8. Nature creates land via volcanic activity, earthquakes, landslides, typhoons, and hurricanes.
9.   Nature takes land away via earthquakes, volcanoes, landslides, typhoons, and hurricanes.
10.   Humans' behavior does not influence the climate of the earth!

These are all facts. It is also true that many don't stop and think about these logical facts. When the media, politicians, teachers, and celebutards all cry out together on TV to save the planet, save the trees, and save the oceans, many of us fall for their lies. These mind-numbed individuals are just reading a prepared script without actually taking the time to find the truth. Just keep in mind that actors read scripts for a living. When it comes to reality, the closest

Hollywood types come to reality is when they star in a reality show. Yet, for some reason, these famous celebrities seem to know more than we do, and they are out there spreading lies about us killing the planet. If we really were killing the planet, we would see a huge increase in the cost of food. Crops would stop growing and animals would be dropping dead of starvation. We would notice if our planet were dying! Maybe if you live in a third world country, you may think the earth is dying. Most damage to the environment is done in communist countries, third world countries, and overreaching governments.

☐☐

With the help of lobbyists and environmentalists, our government is doing all they can to damage people's lives and our environment. Most Americans know nothing about the "DEAD ZONE" in the Gulf of Mexico. A dead zone occurs when there is hypoxia, or oxygen-depleted water. These low levels of oxygen are believed to have been caused by pollution from farm fertilizers as they empty into rivers and eventually the Gulf. Thanks to Congress, millions of acres of sea life have perished largely because of greedy environmentalists, lobbyists, and politicians. Congress is forcing oil companies to use bio-fuels and add ethanol to our fuel to save the environment. Because of ethanol, farmers have to plant twice as many crops of corn to produce enough food and ethanol. They use twice as much fertilizer and pesticide to grow twice as many crops. Not only is this causing driving people in 3rd world nations to eat dirt, these fertilizers also wash into the Mississippi river and flow into the Gulf of Mexico killing everything and, creating the giant Dead Zone.☐

There is plenty of proof that ethanol harms the environment, yet Congress insists it is helping. It has also been proven to harm smaller engines, decrease our MPG, and increase the price of food and energy. Congress insists that it is safe, and they believe this will get us off fossil fuels. Even though it takes one and a half barrels of fossil fuel to make one barrel of ethanol, now, they are making us use more fossil fuels to make ethanol. The Department of Energy and the Department of Agriculture are taking billions of dollars out of our pockets to subsidize ethanol, a failing additive that is actually damaging our environment. Thanks to these two departments, our food and fuel costs thrice as much as they would have had these departments never existed. This is why it's important that we close these controlling authorities. The cost of gasoline would be under $1/gallon in one year if the federal government closed the Department of Energy. With these and other departments shut down, we could lift the poor out of poverty and feed the starving children around the world!

It has been proven repeatedly that the private sector protects the environment much better than any government-run agency at about 20% of what it costs the government. The private sector knows how to preserve and capitalize on the environment better than the government ever will. Simply put, the federal government should not be involved. The private sector creates a beautiful environment, while governments destroy environments.

So how do we control the environment? How do we stop the

seas from rising and the globe from warming? The answer is we don't. We must live around the environment and buy insurance. We have to adapt to whatever changes come our way, for we cannot stop them. They are Mother Nature's will whether it's beaches washing away or rivers flooding and washing towns and cities away. We can find several cities in Greece, which are under the oceans, most likely because Mother Nature decided to change the landscape. On earth, land is giveth, and land is taketh away by Mother Nature and God. This happens in the form of a storm, an earthquake, or a volcanic eruption. It is Mother Nature who ultimately decides what will be preserved. We cannot predict or control what part of our planet will experience these natural disasters caused by nature. At this time, the only real disaster that we can stop is the impact of a meteor hitting the earth. Thanks to the advances of modern technology, we can very likely stop such disasters from occurring and wiping out the human race. To save us all from meteor impact would take the cooperation of all nations, working together for one common cause. Other than that, when Mother Nature comes knocking, make sure you have insurance and you are not stranded in a third world country.

It's obvious that we have no control of the global environment, but we do have control over our local environment. To clean up the local environment around us, we must spread capitalism and free markets all over the world. Free markets create wealth, and wealth creates clean environments and emphasizes the protection of our environment. If you don't believe this, just visit any country in South America and drink a glass of tap water. The truth about the environment is right in front of us. Just take a look at any third world country (but not the resort areas!). Walk down the average street. There, you will see how poor nations with corrupt governments treat the environment. You will NOT find many clean streets or sanitary living conditions for the poor in these countries. You will find deforesting without replanting and many who couldn't care less about the environment. They kill the forest and wildlife by torching thousands of acres. They have no concern for endangered species or protected forests. It shows just how serious environmentalists are about the environment and endangered species. The world does not have the proper leadership to stop these poor nations from destroying their land. The United Nations is supposed to stop evil governments that hold the faith of the natural wonders, yet the UN does nothing. Sometimes, big name celebrities throw rock concerts (e.g., Live Aid, Band Aid, Farm Aid) in the name of saving the environment and helping people in these third world nations. All of this has done absolutely no good for the environment or the people they are supposed to help. People are still dying in Africa, farmers are still struggling, and the planet is still the same, but governments have grown larger and have destroyed more lives. Only capitalism can clean everyone's environment and truly provide a decent life for all of humankind and nature's creatures around the world. □

□

What about the global environment? Am I hurting it? Am I polluting? The answer is no. You have as much of an effect on the global environment as you do when you pee in the ocean. Live your life to the fullest, be successful at what you do, and speak the word of God, speak the truth. Wealthy capitalist nations create clean and beautiful environments because people who earn honest livings and have disposable incomes can and will create lush landscapes and beautiful yards with many trees, plants, and gardens. We all see how crowded Home Depot or Lowes gets on a Sunday, with people going to buy things to beautify their homes, yards, and neighborhoods. This is what capitalist nations do. They create beauty and innovation.

□□

Let's save the planet, save our environment, and get the federal government control out of our environment! Call, fax, or email your representative and demand that they close all federal departments and help protect our freedom and the environment! Visit www.destructivepolitics.com and email Congress to close the federal departments starting with the Department of Energy!

====================
Chapter 3 – Health Care
====================

There is a simple and easy solution to fixing healthcare in the United States. If Congress can implement these four rules, we could solve the healthcare problem within one year and everyone will have access to affordable healthcare.

Health Care and Health Insurance Reform Bill

1. Lift, end and ban every government mandate, which is aimed at the medical industry.

2. Lift, end and ban any government control over private insurance companies' right to sell insurance across state lines.

3. Tort reform. Cap every medical-related lawsuit.

4. Health Insurance Savings Accounts

U nder government management, universal healthcare will KILL our parents and grandparents. It will also cause irreparable damages to people who are suffering from non-life threatening, but still serious, injuries. Rationing treatment is what government-run universal healthcare leads to. No matter where it is tried, it is a failure. In nations like England and Canada, people suffering must wait years for treatment they often never get. The position in line for treatment in these countries is not determined by the severity of your case; it is determined by your age and your status in society, people ahead of you in line, among other complex requirements. Under universal healthcare, a bureaucrat thousands of miles away determines when you will be treated, not your doctor. When care is rationed, it creates the situation where non-life threatening injuries can become catastrophic due to delay of treatment. This is how universal healthcare function.

□□

How can anyone make an accusation like this about universal healthcare? Because it is the truth and it has been proven repeatedly in every country that currently carries universal healthcare. Nations with universal healthcare are nations with substandard healthcare, which causes thousands of people to suffer and loose their lives every year. The survival rate for patients suffering from terminal sickness or injury is over 50% higher in the U.S. than in most nations with socialized universal healthcare! Just look at survival rate of patients suffering from prostate cancer or breast cancer in Great Britain, Germany, France, or Canada. More people survive in the U.S. than in other industrialized nations on earth. By learning about the quality of their socialized universal healthcare, we can take a glimpse into our future. We can see what could happens if the U.S. government forced universal healthcare on us. France has Universal Care, in the summer of 2003 in France, nearly 20,000 seniors died of heat stroke. Government-controlled healthcare left these people to die. Some speculate it was because the doctors were on vacation and getting them back for an emergency would have been costly for the government. □

□

Currently, Canadian healthcare is also having problems, it is failing its citizens hence Canadians seek aid in the US. If the U.S. were not bordering Canada, tens of thousands of Canadians would be crippled or dead because of their own government-controlled healthcare inefficiencies. The Canadian healthcare system is so inefficient that government decided allow private practices to open, this is helping correct some of the problems caused by government. In Canada, for an additional out of pocket fee, citizens are now able to get quality treatment without having to wait for years through the universal government system. Like every other nation on earth, the state-run healthcare cannot provide for its citizens as properly and efficiently as private companies. Canadian healthcare system is over whelmed by patients to the point that Canada must to rely on private care physicians for an out of pocket expense. The Canadian government still limits the number of private care physicians to just a few provinces even thought there is a need for more. To top it off, the government ensured that private practices must abide by the failed Canadian Health Act, which states that privately run facilities cannot charge citizens for services covered by government insurance. In the real world, when governments have total control of healthcare, they destroy whatever good was in healthcare before they got involved. As with everything which functions properly in the world, the private sector is what corrects the inefficiencies caused by bureaucrats in governments. The private sector can make it better because they are driven by profits and competition. The better they treat patients, the more patients will come for private care, therefore creating a profit and self-enrichment, which is what we all want in life. The government does not care about any of this. To the government, we are just a number, and no bureaucrat will ever care if we live or die! If the government messes up, you can't sue for their mistakes.

□□

We are in danger in America. Congress successfully passed the universal healthcare program in November 2009. If the Senate passes this bill, every American citizen will suffer Because Obama will sign it, he signs anything that Pelosi or Reid put in front of him. With the exception of government employees, every American will be mandated to use substandard government healthcare. One of the most alarming features of this healthcare bill threatens our way of life and our freedom via fines and jail time. The bill Congress voted on in November 2009 states that if we do not buy government mandated health insurance; we can end up in jail. Our lives and our futures were determined behind closed doors by a handful of lawyers and lobbyists lead by Nancy Pelosi in Washington, D.C. This group of politicians, lawyers and lobbyists are planning to revamp our entire healthcare industry and place it into the hands of tens of thousands of bureaucrats. People who contributed to this health care bill also authored books, which advocate population control. When the federal government runs healthcare, bureaucrats will determine what age group will be sacrificed or depending on who is in power, what religion or race will be rationed. Our leaders in Congress are misguided and in pursuit of total power and control over every aspect of our lives. These very same leaders ignore the catastrophic failures of universal healthcare in England, Canada, Germany, Italy, or any other nation on earth. Our Congress is also ignoring the fraud and mismanagement in Medicare, Medicaid, Social Security, the Department of Energy, the Department of Education, and every other government-run agency. Members of Congress didn't even bother reading the 2,000 page healthcare bill they voted to pass! While not having read the bill or knowing what is in the bill, our leaders in Congress have the audacity to tell us we don't know any better, and they call Americans "teabaggers" and organized protesters. They look at us like we, the people, are stupid and we do not understand. The most offensive thing about this is that politicians are arguing with us and trying to convince us that this bill is what we need to better our lives even though most of them have not even read the bill. Who has time to read a 2,000 page bill when they are busy printing and spending money?

Of all the nations which use universal healthcare, not one has a healthcare system that is equal to or as good as that of the U.S. In fact, when leaders of any nation in the world need complicated surgery, they don't go to hospitals in their own country; they choose an American hospital. The average citizens of Canada, Britain, Europe, and nations around the world are forced into their own government-controlled healthcare system. Under these systems, people are subject to rationalized healthcare. Many are dying because their government rationed healthcare to the point that there is simply not enough care to go around. Cases have been made where British citizens enter a government-run hospital and they end up getting even sicker than they were when they went in. Great Britain's Health Secretary Alan Johnson had to apologize in Parliament in 2007, as it was reported that at least 90 patients in southeast England died as a result of infections they picked up in the hospital. The British government-run healthcare is in such disarray that many patients end up getting infected with deadly diseases they never had before entering the hospital.

When a bureaucrat decides that your condition costs too much to cure, or it does not meet some complex criteria you will be neglected and left to wither away and die! This is the Democratic universal healthcare in Canada and England, and this is what our own government is trying to force upon us. Don't let Obama and Pelosi care neglect your parents and your grandparents. No matter how congress try to word it, whether they call it "insurance reform," "government competing with private insurance," or "healthcare reform," it is all the same government-run healthcare at the end. Our mainstream media is also lying to us by not investigating and looking into the truth about universal healthcare. When you choose to let government run healthcare, you will find yourself with second-class healthcare. You will end up in a dirty government-run hospital and probably see your condition worsen instead of improve. We can see this in Canada, Europe, and even in our veterans' hospitals here in America. Government-run hospitals become terrible incubators of germs and diseases, thereby increasing the number of people who need more treatment.

☐

In the US, we find badly managed healthcare where government is in charge. The Washington Post, in February 2007, told of a whole list of problems at "Building 18." This building was once a motel, but was converted to a long-term outpatient dormitory at the Washington hospital. The Washington Post found troops who lost limbs and suffered very serious traumatic brain injuries or post-traumatic stress from the war were being mistreated in these VA hospitals. These brave soldiers who risked their lives in combat now had to risk their lives in a government-run hospital where they were quartered for months in moldy and rodent-infested rooms with inadequate follow-up care.

When discovered, the panel chairman, Rep. John Tierney, called "the unsanitary conditions" and other problems at Walter Reed Hospital "appalling." Appalling? How about disrespectful? How can our Congress allow this to happen and at the same time advocate the same kind of healthcare for the rest of us citizens? ☐

☐

Imagine if you sacrificed your life for this nation by confronting evil terrorists and communists on the battlefield and you were injured. Then, you come home to be treated in a government-run hospital, only to have your condition worsen. We don't have to go very far in our own country to see just how mismanaged healthcare will be if the federal government is in charge.

In early 2009, we learned of the SARS bird flu. In Toronto, SARS was spread through an unsanitary government-run hospital infecting staff and unsuspecting patients. This Toronto hospital became an incubator for SARS and spread the disease from Toronto all the way to upstate New York. This is what happens with government-run hospitals under universal care. Basic hygiene procedures are cut just for the sake of cutting costs. Congress tells us socialized healthcare will save us money and treat everyone, but the government-run hospitals never have enough needles, bandages, or other necessities to actually treat everyone. This happens because there is a thick layer of bureaucracy and most of the money goes to administration fees instead of the sick patients. The evidence is simply overwhelming, and it is appalling that our Congress does not take time to investigate this. The federal government will have to hire over 50,000 new bureaucrats to manage all the Americans who will be enrolled in universal care. These bureaucrats will command an average somewhere around $60,000 a year. That alone will cost the federal government hundreds of millions of dollars a year. This money will be taken out of necessities in hospitals and clinics.☐

☐

We can not fall for Obama or Pelosi's lies and tricks. They told us we are too incompetent to handle our own healthcare. Barack Obama and Nancy Pelosi, who have never worked in the healthcare industry, are rapidly assembling a universal healthcare with a team of trial lawyers and lobbyists. Do we want a group of lawyers to decide what healthcare should be like and who should be treated? These are the same lawyers who deliberately avoid discussing tort reform, the root cause of the rising cost of healthcare. Tort reform is not in the healthcare bill because lawyers earn their hundreds of millions of dollars every year by suing doctors. When a lawyer wins an exorbitant lawsuit, the cost of insurance for doctors goes up, and every American is stuck paying more money for their healthcare. Why is no one in Washington, D.C. asking the question, how can a pack of lawyers and politicians fix our healthcare if they never worked in the healthcare industry? Wouldn't doctors be better qualified to fix healthcare? Yes, they would, and if Congress listened to doctors, they would discover that the real way to bring cost of healthcare down is to deal with tort reform first.

□□

President Obama was greeted by a disappointed crowd in June 2009 when he spoke at the annual meeting of the American Medical Association in Chicago. He was booed by a group, which included America's leading medical experts. Why were they booing him so much? He was booed because President Obama, whose allegiance lies with the trial lawyers, declared that he was "not advocating caps on malpractice awards." These medical experts know a whole lot more about the cost of healthcare than President Obama and Nancy Pelosi know or will ever know. Yet still, Obama insisted that tort reform is not going to be discussed because it is not relevant to healthcare reform.

It costs billions of dollars and takes thousands of valuable hours for a medical practitioner to protect himself or herself against malpractice lawsuits. Because of so many lawsuits, doctors are running more tests than necessary to make sure they don't overlook the slightest problem. This is running up the cost of medicine in our country. President Barack Obama referred to the cost of "unnecessary tests and procedures as part of a 'defensive' medicine culture created in part by the risk of medical malpractice lawsuits." He even called the runaway cost of healthcare "a threat to our economy." He also declared it "a ticking time-bomb." Yet this ticking time bomb is one he is not willing to defuse. It is obvious that doctors are doing unnecessary tests because they know if they happen to overlook one slight detail, they will find themselves in a courtroom with an overzealous lawyer ready to cash in on a jackpot lawsuit. Spending time in court takes medical practitioners away from where they should be in the office curing sick patients. □

□

Unfortunately, the legal lobby is the most powerful lobby group in Congress with more influence on our leaders than any other group. This ensures that tort reform will not happen and that the cost of healthcare will keep on rising no matter what Congress does. Until we have tort reform, we will not have affordable healthcare.

If universal government-controlled healthcare is the answer to all our problems, then why won't anyone in Congress opt out of their current plan and enroll in this universal plan? Because this universal plan is not good enough for them or their pets. If it's not good enough for Congress, then it's not good enough for us! We, the taxpayers, are currently paying for the best quality healthcare Congress currently enjoys! Yet these ungrateful, leaders take this for granted and look down on taxpayers as if we were their servants in a monarchy. Pelosi and Obama believe we should be happy with what they give us. If Congress is going to force government healthcare on us, then we should force government healthcare on Congress!

☐

Obama is telling us universal government-controlled healthcare will bring in competition and quality healthcare. That is 100% false, a lie. Just look at Great Britain or Canada. Repeatedly, we hear horror stories from Canadians about how horrible their federal government-controlled mandated healthcare is. The United States of America is saving thousands of Canadian lives every year just by bordering Canada. If the United States goes by way of Canadian-style government-mandated healthcare, thousands of Canadians will die! Citizens will be refused healthcare on the basis of cost and their contribution to society. Government will look at a patient's lifestyle and if the patient had a healthy diet and exercised or not. This is how they will save money for the government by blaming you for your irresponsible lifestyle and choosing to deny healthcare based on how you lived your life. This will help the federal government save money on Medicare, Medicaid, and Social Security. Note how the Democrats approach fixing healthcare and the budget by rationing healthcare for the citizens. This means you and your loved ones! This is how Nancy Pelosi and Barack Obama plan to save the country from going bankrupt.

☐☐

Our biggest problems with healthcare are created by the federal government. The high costs, the long waits are due to government involvement. Just imagine what your life would be like if, at your job, you had to get government approval for every decision you made.

-If you ran a restaurant, you would have to get the government to approve your menu, your prices, how you cook the food, how you serve the food, what kind of spoons you must use to cook, what the oven temperature should be, and so on.

-If you were a mechanic, you would have to run every job you were to perform past a government bureaucrat before you could start the procedure to change a transmission, to change an engine, to fix brakes, or change tires!

You would have to get approval from a bureaucrat in the government for everything you wanted to fix or do. This is what doctors have to deal with now, and it will get even worse once universal healthcare becomes law! The federal government is destroying family medicine. It is taking skilled doctors who could be working on the sick and forcing them to deal with frivolous lawsuits, excessive paper work and other obstacles brought on by federal mandates.

The problem is government wants to regulate and decide everything. Unfortunately, they always end up destroying what ever it is they want to regulate. The new regulations create an environment for corruption and theft to flourish, costing tax payers of billions of dollars each year. Federal investigators believe that organized and lucrative schemes bilk Medicare out of an estimated 60 billion dollars a year! Our leaders in the federal government don't seem very keen to do anything to stop it. It is quite possible the special interest groups who are stealing all this money are supporting the leaders in Congress. This can be one explanation for the continued and unchecked corruption happening daily. Where is Nancy Pelosi? Where are our elected officials standing up for our rights as citizens, protecting our hard earned tax money? They should be making sure this kind of fraud does not happen? What are they doing? They are not doing anything to stop the corruption, as too many of their lobbyists' and associates are likely the recipients of all this fraudulent money. Our leaders in Washington are busy making sure the corrupt environment remains. Some of the $60 billion in Medicare fraud money quite possibly ends up in our elected officials' campaigns as contributions. Why else would they not investigate it? Since Congress is more concerned about protecting the lawyers and the status quo, chances are Medicare will remain corrupt.

The legal groups are also hard at work creating more rules and regulations for doctors to adapt. Just take a glance at the 2000 page health care reform bill, if you have 2months! With more rules and regulations, doctors have to spend even more time on paperwork instead of patient work. Congress has caused so many problems that it has become very difficult for new doctors to open a practice. The cost of malpractice insurance alone is so expensive that it drives up the cost of opening an office to practice medicine. This high cost is directly caused by the frivolous lawsuits.

Canadian healthcare is so slow to treat patients that some towns have decided to set up lotteries. If you are lucky enough, and they pull your name, you get surgery and the medical attention you need! This is where America is headed if we do not stop the federal government! They U.S. government has already bankrupted Medicare. The costs of operating Medicare are over seven times what they projected since they started it. Even though the government is spending more on Medicare, the time you spend waiting for treatment and quality of care have not improved. ☐

☐

So what is the solution? To find the answer to fixing our healthcare, let's look at what is proven and what has worked in the past.☐

☐

If we look at corrective eye surgery, liposuctions, nose jobs, or any other cosmetic surgery not covered by most insurances and are not tampered with by the federal government. The price of these procedures has dropped by over 60% in the past 15 years. This is all due to competition and market forces. Unfortunately, the government doesn't think so. They believe they should be in the middle as a mediator. The government believes they can manage the cost of healthcare better than you or private insurance companies even after running up a $13 trillion debt. Anything the government tries to manage is corrupt, and the costs are out of control. There's no need to go far back to see what the federal government has done to healthcare for veterans or Medicare, or what they have done in the state of Massachusetts. How can any reasonable person have any faith in anything that Congress does? The federal government has destroyed the lives of millions of people. We must take the power out of the hands of these elected politicians on Capitol Hill. Why does Washington, D.C. have to be involved in a medical procedure that is taking place in Alaska, or California, or Maine, or Hawaii?

⬜⬜

The Democratic Congress is filled with elitists who think that more government management is what is needed. In Massachusetts, the State government passed a State-run healthcare program to cover the poor who could not afford to get health insurance. The program has been in place for less than five years, and Massachusetts noticed they had no money to treat the ones who needed this care the most. Massachusetts's government decided to kick 20,000 of the poorest people out of the state-run healthcare program in 2009. Not only that, people are estimating that costs of healthcare is going up three times as quickly in Massachusetts than anywhere else in the U.S. This is just a small sample of what is to come all across the United States. If Congress is truly serious about fixing our healthcare, they will start with tort reform and get then work on getting the federal government out of healthcare. The government must let the private sector handle healthcare; there is an important difference between doctors who practice medicine and bureaucrats. Doctors who practice take the Hippocratic oath to save lives, bureaucrats take no oath, yet they will decide if you or your loved ones will get the care he or she desperately needs. That decision should be left up to family members and doctors. The solution is very simple; if we all want affordable healthcare, we must get the federal government out of health care

⬜⬜

For our Congress and President, healthcare is not about taking care of the sick and the poor; it is about taking money away from hardworking Americans. Our government, with Pelosi's leadership collaborated and conspired to have the federal government take over the health insurance industry, by force if necessary. They have calculated that health insurance will cost anywhere from $12,000 to $17,000 a year per American. They are likely counting on over 100 million people to buy health insurance, which can bring well over $1 trillion a year in additional revenues. If you don't believe this whole healthcare bill is a scam to get more money from you, then you do not understand our federal government. We can look at Social Security (BANKRUPT), Medicare (BANKRUPT), or any other government program (BANKRUPT)! The U.S. owes $13 trillion. We have no money for anything, especially hiring more bureaucrats to take more private sector jobs and ruin lives.

With federal healthcare, we will see patient dumping like we have never seen before. Our President Obama's wife has plenty of experience patient dumping. She was partly responsible for a patient-dumping scheme at Chicago University Hospital to cut costs. Under her direction, the hospital purposely turned away poor people with low incomes. The university hospital chose their patients according to the health insurance provider they carried. Most poor people were turned away and sent to local clinics because they had no insurance. Using this method, the university hospital reaped millions of dollars in profits, thereby proving that Michelle Obama is more concerned with profits than helping poor folks who need urgent medical care. Currently, a group of lawyers is working on overhauling our healthcare, and not one Democratic representative has any clue about what is in there. How can a group of lawyers fix healthcare when they and their class action lawsuits are DIRECTLY responsible for the high cost of healthcare? Does anyone here think that doctors are out to be rich and lawyers are looking out for us? Quite the opposite, lawyers are out there looking for any excuse to sue doctors for hundreds of millions of dollars. Case in point, John Edwards is one of the wealthiest class action lawyers in the country. He got there by suing doctors for hundreds of millions.

☐☐

The only way to truly reform healthcare is removing the U.S. government from our healthcare industry. Once that happens, we will see healthcare costs drop substantially along with the cost of medicine and the cost of insurance. We must stop Congress from meddling with our healthcare. Our politicians look down at us citizens while taking our money and punishing us for working hard. They want to separate us and treat taxpayers like second-class citizens. When one of our representatives bought up a bill, which mandated that Congress live with the same universal healthcare they are pushing on us, every single Democrat voted against it. Does this say anything? How can people believe they will get quality healthcare if Congress refuses to take part in any of it? They will destroy and bankrupt healthcare like they destroyed Medicare, Medicaid, Social Security, education, and others. Every single federal program is a disaster, a failure, and an embarrassment. Why is it that not one of these departments is being considered for elimination or thoroughly reviewed by independent non-partisan groups?

☐

We must change this and get government out of healthcare completely. Call, write, or email Congress every day. Send them

100 emails a day if you can and demand that they get out of our lives and let the private sector fix our healthcare. If we can take government out of our healthcare, within one year, we will notice insurance premiums drop and quality of healthcare improve like never before. Don't forget that here in America; we still have the best health care in the world. I can say that confidently because anyone who is important around the world comes to America for complicated surgeries. They don't go to Europe, Asia, or Africa; they come to America because they know we have the best healthcare in the world. It is the best care in the world because healthcare is driven by the private sector, profits and pursuit of success. That will all change if we allow Congress to take over healthcare and slowly push the private sector out. When government runs our health care, we will see new developments and technological advances in medicine come to a standstill. Any incentive to make a better product will be removed because there will be no profit to be made. This in turn will give us substandard healthcare just like the rest of the world.

Its plain and simple, any country with government run health care is facing a disaster in the making. The federal government should not run our healthcare! They have proven to be irresponsible and destroyed too many lives by tampering with our Medicare.☐Visit www.destructivepolitics.com email Congress and demand they stop Universal Healthcare!

Chapter 4 – Religion

"Those who speak the truth speak the word of God."

G OD IS TRUTH! Yes, truth, the truth we speak. God is not some ghost or spirit. God is not someone looking over you and taking notes every time you curse, lie, cheat, or steal. Nor is God waiting around for your prayers of winning lotto numbers or having everything work out right in your life. God helps those who help themselves! That means if you don't get up and do what makes you happy, then God will not help you.☐ ☐

We can pray for world peace; we can pray to end world hunger and feed the starving children; we can pray to end genocide; we can pray for things to work out or whatever we desperately want or desire. Unless we take the initiative to make it happen, chances are our prayers will not be answered. If we don't stop the aggressive nations, terrorists, and gangs that attack innocent people, then there won't be peace in the world. The poor, the weak, and the innocent will go hungry for another decade or longer. If we don't deliver food to the starving children, they will not have anything to eat, and they will starve to death. This is truth, God is truth! Those who create the turbulent environment are evil; they must be dealt with before evil eventually deals with us.

Imagine for a moment, of the six billion people on this planet, at least half of those people are praying for something. Some pray for wealth, fame, or success, while some pray for Jihad and some pray to exterminate certain races and religions. Some pray for good grades or a new job, some pray for a better life, some pray to get off death row, and some pray for ice cream. YES! You don't think children pray? It goes on and on and on. You can go to church seven days a week, get on your knees, and beg… Then, ask yourself this. To whom are you begging for help? To whom are you asking for forgiveness? To whom are you asking to give you a better life? At the end of it all, you are having an honest conversation with yourself, and perhaps, at that moment, on your knees, you open up to yourself and discover your faults. That is God talking to you, to help you look within yourself.

If you truly want forgiveness, ask the people you wronged how you can get them to forgive you for what you've done. If you want Jihad, prepare to be stopped by the army of God, the U.S. Military and allies! If you want good grades, put down the Xbox and Play Station and learn about the subject in which you want good grades! Do you want a new job? Go out and network, meet people, look in the classifieds, talk to friends, and you will find a good job. If you want a better life, it's up to you to make it happen. If you wait for someone to give you a better life, you will live a life as a slave to government, just like the people in North Korea, the old Soviet Union, or Nazi Germany!

Don't expect God to come to your house and magically make your life better or get you a pay raise at work; those things are up to you! You just have to make sure you do the right things in life. When you live your life as honestly and as truthfully as you can, your life will be good to you. The dreams and goals you set for yourself will be within reach, and the only obstacle will be your self. This is what made the United States such a powerful nation the freedom that God gave us to be the best that we can be. With this freedom, we must be responsible. As parents, we should raise our children to respect their elders. As good citizens, we must ensure that evil governments do not push God out of our lives and give us evil corrupt government like it happened all through history. God gave us tools to accomplish anything we put our minds to. These tools are talents, the ability to speak and communicate clearly, to comprehend, to remember, and to make logical decisions. In America, we decide our faith. We are free to go anywhere we want and pursue any goals and dreams we set for ourselves. This is truth. This is what our founding fathers gave us, a nation guided by truth.

The rule of law guided by truth is what government must live by and up hold. In the year 2010 America, the rule of law is decided by one government official on capital hill, she is the Speaker of The House of Representatives. Leaders, no matter how powerful are not always truthful.

When we are governed by truth, we are free, and we can be the best at what we do without one person in government tampering with our lives. We should all be aware of the invisible hand of the federal government, for it can become the hand, which can harm us for generations. This invisible hand destroys countless lives with the stroke of a pen. The deceptive ways of the federal government will get people hooked on government handouts. In time government will ask for things in return, wealth and valuables, then eventually our children. This is where powerful governments inevitably lead; they will create drafts and indoctrinate our children, train them and use them for protection against us.

In a free nation ruled by laws and God, our leaders are not despised, for they cannot manipulate our lives. In free nations, people can be what they want to be, free to build, design, invent, create or manufacture whatever they dream of. It's up to us to make our lives a better place and decide our own destiny, not the governments. □The success of America was possible because we had a small government that was not overly burdening to its citizens. As long as we have a fair and free environment with limited federal government interference, we can enjoy a beautiful and plentiful life. It is truth that gave us the wealth and prosperity we enjoy today, it is lies by the federal government, which will take them away.

□□

The lies in our society come in the form of an overbearing government, spreading lies and evil. This evil creeps its way into every society and nation on earth because people let their guards down. This evil disguises itself as fair and just by treating everyone equally, but in reality, it does no such thing. The evils of socialism place a few manipulating, powerful elitists in positions of power to rule over all with no regard for the consequences of their destructive decisions. These evil powers overtake us, it comes in many forms; socialism, liberalism, environmentalism, progressives, communism, Nazi, Monarchy, fascists or what ever new catchy label they choose. For hundreds of years, they have changed the names around to appeal to a few who do not know, but at the end of it all, it's another form of government control perpetrated by a few elitists in power. Like thousands of years before, the evil power and the lies of socialist governments and kings eventually overreach and attempt to force God out of our lives. Today, our government spreads lies and organizes citizens to echo these lies. They repeatedly inject hatred and class envy between the rich and poor. These are the kinds of actions governments do to slowly break nations down, eventually remove God from peoples lives, and replace it with falsehoods, lies perpetrated by evil, powerful central governments.

God is always with us, and if we work hard, we will succeed at what we set out to accomplish, as God will reward us. America is filled with success stories of individuals who were honest and hardworking. By pursuing their own dreams, they opened the door of opportunity for thousands of others and created wealth through honest hard work. This is the environment God creates through capitalism— an atmosphere of truth where individuals conduct honest business between one another regardless of race, religion or ethnicity. These people in pursuit of happiness accomplish incredible things. On their way to enrich themselves, these individuals create a ripple of success through the economy. We saw many people like this awaken when this nation was founded. We removed all the lies, and evil, the shackles that kings, warlords, socialists, and powerful rulers had over God-loving people for the past thousands of years. America is successful because truth was allowed to prevail, we had fair contract laws, and we were free to create, invent, and prosper and take that prosperity and wealth and spread it around the world the way God intended.

America spreads its wealth, liberates and feeds nations all over the world. We reached a level of success that has never been seen before. This environment guided by god flourished in America due to low taxes and a small federal government. It is undeniable that when taxes are low, America gives more money to charity than anyone else in the world. It is God's will that those who have more than they need will eventually give much of it away. On the other hand, when governments forcefully take wealth from people by raising their taxes, then people will do what they can to protect their wealth, they will also hold back their charitable contributions. This happens because people don't know how much more the government will eventually take from them. It's not government's place to tell you how to spread your wealth if you earned it! If you worked hard and earned a lot of money, you should decide how much you want to give away, not the federal government.

Now more than ever, it is becoming clearer why God is so important in our lives. Without God, our nation has no meaning and will eventually fall into chaos like third world nations. Countries all around the world are run by the kind of leaders our founding fathers feared, escaped from, and fought against. The leaders of these nations share the same state of mind as leaders who oppressed their citizens through lies and threats hundreds of years ago. With no truth in their nations and nothing but lies on top of lies, God vanished from people's lives and prayers were left unanswered. God will show you a difficult life if you live under the rule of dictators and communists, as evident in places like North Korea, Haiti and Iran. These of godless societies exist because of a few thugs who are forcing lies upon their citizens via threats and the use of deadly force. When evil takes precedence in societies, trust disappears and people become defensive and paranoid, eventually they stop trusting each other and spread lies about each other. When trust no longer exists in a society, businesses begin fail because deceptive criminal acts will begin to rise. This is what happens to all godless societies. Life soon becomes a fight for survival instead of a joy of living. How can anyone enjoy life when you don't know what is true and what is a lie?

☐

This is slowly happening in America in 2009. Our government under the leadership of Barack Obama, Nancy Pelosi, and Harry Reid is dividing this nation and creating class envy through lies and deception. They are hurting our lives by deceiving and delivering more evil government control and regulation. To understand the contrast between the Democrats and conservative Republicans, let's compare the two. God and commonsense will help you decide which one cares about your life. To illustrate, in Chart 1, I included a well-known conservative Republican from the 1980s, Ronald Reagan and our Democratic liberal socialist President, Barack

Obama. Naturally, we can use whatever tools we need to compare and understand the stark contrast between the two and the way both of them affect your life. See chart1

chart 1

Ronald Reagan (R)   Barack Obama (D)

Ronald Reagan (R)	Barack Obama (D)
Inherited a recession caused by Jimmy Carter and Democrats	Inherited a recession caused by Nancy Pelosi and Democrats
Believed in individuals	Believes in government
Said big government was evil and corrupt	Said private companies were greedy and corrupt
Cut taxes	Raised taxes
Slowed the growth of government	Added 200,000 employees to government in his first year
Opposed dictators, Marxists, communists	Supports dictators, Marxists, communists
Spoke from the heart	Speaks from the teleprompter
When people look at Reagan or hear his name, they think of optimism and freedom	When people look at Obama, they think of pessimism, lies, indebted servitude, and dark days ahead

When a nation is based on nothing but lies, people can't live an honest life because they don't know what's real. Without God, nations will eventually meet their demise. This usually happens to socialist nations because, in time, all the lies break down the way society functions. It is very important that we stay as honest as we can and we elect honest leaders, for they are the ones who are going to decide our faith, and they are the ones who speak the word of God for us. Nobody wants to be lied to!

☐

History is filled with rulers, warlords, and powerful religious groups who constantly lied and forced people to live under their rules or convert in the name of a God. These aggressive groups never spoke the word of God, for they enslaved their newly concurred people and took their territory. Even the church has not always spoken the word of God. Just a few hundred years ago, the church was forcing religion onto people all around the world in the name of God. To accomplish this, they often murdered and tortured thousands of innocent people. That was not God sending out the armies to murder, conquer, and force people to convert; that was the governments, occasionally with the blessing of the pope. This was the dominating and concurring attitude all across Europe and much of the world for thousands of years. The rule by force and oppression was the way of the world, not much has changed. There are still many parts of the world where God does not participate, and where many nations will jail and torture you if you speak the truth.

□□

In the past 1000 years, America has been the only nation that created a system of government, which is fair to all in the eyes of God. Our founders created this government with truth guiding them every step of the way. The past gave them much guidance as to how to frame our constitution and bill of rights. These documents are responsible for our God-given freedom, for everything in these documents is true. If people in government tamper with these documents today, we will decent into a dark, enslaving future. With no God in our lives, governments will take full control of our destinies and turn us into slaves. Our founders did what they could to ensure the federal government would not control us.

To make America "The Shining City On The Hill," as Ronald Reagan described America; our founders recognized that a powerful government would eventually become an obstacle in people's lives. It is why they gave limited powers to the federal government and no rights for government to control our behaviors. In the minds of our founders, limited government gave us unlimited access to God. This is what made America the shining city on the hill, the nation in which the whole world has placed its trust. In the past, the U.S. government did not interfere with commerce to the level other governments did in other countries around the world. Government was not regulating energy, food, education, labor, gun ownership, or anything business-related. This is what made America a great country, it was enterprising individuals, pioneers and risk takers who helped shape this great nation. With no strict government control and god guiding the way, America advanced faster than any other nation in history. In 200 short years, our standard of living surpassed that of every other nation on this planet! Our length of life, healthcare, and treatment of our elderly surpassed that of every other nation in history! People were inventing, creating, and innovating like never before people like Henry Ford, the Wright brothers, and many others. This happened because government was not restricting and micromanaging people's lives. Under the rules of God, people were free to pursue their dreams and use their God-given talents to accomplish amazing things. Average everyday people living in all parts of the country were he brilliant minds creating technological advances. These advances employed and enriched the lives of millions all over the world. This is how God spreads wealth and prosperity through capitalism and by giving people the talents to create and innovate. □□

God's will is for governments to have limited powers over the individual rights because it's individuals who make all the good things that happen in this country and the world. Today, our government has become ruthless and cruel; they have been lying to us and trying to mislead us over and over. In essence, our federal government has become Godless. Our politicians demand more and more money so they can create a socialist government-controlled life, like the old Soviet Union. They use government departments to restrict our freedoms and spread lies. Department by department, they control us and manipulate the price of everything we depend on. These departments are like the hand of evil wrapped around America's neck, choking freedom out of our lives. Each and every federal department is a Godless violation of our constitution. Our government will be very reluctant to give up these departments, for they are the source of the powers Congress use to manipulate and control our lives. To government, these evil departments are like a drug, and politicians are hooked on them. They will lie, cheat, and steal; they will do whatever they can to keep these departments open. We can spread the word of God and get these departments out of our lives so we can live free again. Closing all these departments can answer all our prayers and bring back our jobs, 401ks, homes, cars, and everything we lost under the rule of Pelosi, Obama, and Reid. These departments do the work of evil: they spread lies about private sector businesses and they manipulate food production, energy outflow, quality of education, quality of healthcare, taxes, finance, and so on. The lies these departments spread are all confirmed just by looking at our national debt $13 trillion and rapidly growing.☐ All departments are responsible for every dollar wasted in the $13 trillion debt; these departments are the invisible hands of an evil and corrupt government.☐

Committee on Agriculture

Committee on Appropriations

Committee on Armed Services

Committee on the Budget

Committee on Education and Labor

Committee on Energy and Commerce

Committee on Financial Services

Committee on Foreign Affairs

Committee on Homeland Security

Committee on House Administration

Committee on the Judiciary

Committee on Natural Resources

Committee on Oversight and Government Reform

Committee on Rules

Committee on Science and Technology

Committee on Small Business

Committee on Standards of Official Conduct

Committee on Transportation and Infrastructure

Committee on Veterans' Affairs

Committee on Ways and Means

Joint Economic Committee

Joint Congressional Committee on Inaugural Ceremonies

Joint Committee on Taxation

House Permanent Select Committee on Intelligence

House Select Committee on Energy Independence and Global Warming

By closing all these departments, control over our lives and our finances will be removed from the greedy claws of our evil federal government. All the lobbyists, politicians, and lawyers will once again become powerless against us. God will shine through and freedom will once again make this nation as great as it was in the beginning. Now, it's more clear than ever that our freedoms have been tampered with using federal departments in Washington D.C. The root of all the lies and evil in our lives is the overbearing, invisible control of the federal government. To take the evil out and bring truth back to our nations capital, we must strip the federal government of the powers they hold over us. These are the powers they use to control us and hurt all of us, but most of us don't even realize because we have become so accustomed to them. Ours is a nation with a constitution, which specifically emphasizes "limited government intrusion." Our founders risked their lives for America god was by their side very step of the way. By bringing knowledge of history and truth, our founders opened the door for God-loving, freedom-seeking people from all corners of the world. In the name of God, we must stop evil government departments from destroying more lives. Evil governments are responsible for more deaths around the world than any other groups or people. We can look at China under Mao Tse Toung (estimated to have killed up to 70 million Chinese) or Germany under Hitler (killed over 6 million Jews). How about Stalin (murdered over 20 million Russians) or the Cambodia killing fields (over 1million educated intellectuals murdered)? What God allowed all these massacres to take place? It was not God that murdered all those people; it was the evil lies of the governments and dictators. This is the handy work of evil governments. This is the handy work of the devil. When people allow one person to become so powerful that lives become worthless, everyone's life is in danger!

Visit www.destructivepolitics.com and email Congress to close all the evil corrupt departments, the root of all-evil in Washington D.C. starting with the Department of Energy.

Chapter 5 – History

"Those who ignore the past will fall victim to a punishing and unforgiving future. Left unchecked, our government will surely take away all our freedoms and enslave us in time."

In the 1400s, an Aztec king organized a four-day sacrifice by butchering over 80,000 prisoners in just 10 days. The king had shifts of priests four at a time cutting out the prisoners beating hearts while they were held down. With hearts cut out, lifeless bodies were tossed down the blood-drenched pyramid. From Europe to Asia to America, the world was filled with senseless barbaric butchery and the rule of a powerful few that lived above the law or created laws the people had to live by. There was no safe place on this planet for truth or justice to prevail. When we look back in history, we will find that every continent had a violent history full of hardship, tyranny, and slavery.

Not much had changed before America was colonized; the progress of the world was slow and often disrupted by war and oppression. There was conflict almost everywhere with just about everyone the English, the French, the Spanish, the Italians, the Hungarians, the Germans, the Koreans, the Mongolians, the Turks, the Arabs, Catholics, Muslims, Huns, and Romans. You name it; there was a war about to break out somewhere. Powerful warlords and religions were on a quest to conquer as much of the world as they could get their hands on. European nations were constantly at war with each other, confiscating people's wealth, murdering citizens, burning down villages, and colonizing the rest of the world. There was no concern over casualties of war or civilian targets. The wars of the past were bloody and brutal; innocent were slaughtered villages, and towns were burnt to the ground and women and children were not spared. Around the world, entire civilizations were erased from history due to the aggressive use of force. Like before, the world today is filled with senseless violence. Today, terrorists and dictators threaten world peace on several continents.

Our founding fathers were aware of the ruthless nature of kings, dictators, warlords, and other forms of rule by one person or a small group of people. History clearly shows that no one man or group can be trusted with people's freedoms and rights. This is why our founders decided that we must live by the rule of law, not the rule of one powerful man. Our founders understood that a nation built on just laws is the key to a long-lasting, peaceful society. They concluded the path to individual freedom is not in the hands of governments or kings; it is and forever will be in the hands of people guided by fair and just laws that apply equally to everyone, from powerful leaders to citizens. In the past, kings, warlords, dictators, and czars who were not subject to the laws of their people ruled the world. Many of these leaders were selected because they were the next in line in the family. This is still happening today in parts of the world like Cuba, North Korea, and other nations run by kings or dictators. Just like in the past, the power over the people is handed down to next of kin. In the past, this was normal because most people did not know any better. Unfortunately for citizens, many leaders were ruthless and unforgiving and got their way using violence and threats. With the exception of America, to be born in the past was like playing winning the lottery. If you were born to a wealthy family, chances were you were going to live a comfortable life. If you were born to a poor family, chances were you stayed poor for life. The class system was brutal and relentless. Slavery was a normal and accepted way of life in many parts of the world.

□□

Our founders saw this way of life as a threat to humanity, and they understood the dangers of power being handed down the family line of rulers. They learned from history that the fairest system of government is a Republic. A republic treats everyone equally and limits the powers of government. A Republic can stand the test of time as long as our politicians don't corrupt it and destroy it. The constitution of the United States was constructed with all this in mind. The founders studied history and were familiar with the turbulent past of the world. They authored the United States constitution and gave us the representative Republic we live with today. The word Republic originated from a Greek by the name of Solin around 600 BC. Solin urged the creation of a fixed body of laws not subject to majority whims. Sadly, the Greeks never adopted Solin's wise advice as he intended it; the Romans, on the other hand, did. Based on what they knew of Solin, they created Roman laws around Solin's laws and in time built a powerful Republic that limited the power of government and left the people alone. Because government was limited, the people were free to pursue their dreams; they were also allowed to keep the fruits of their labor. In time, Rome became wealthy and the envy of the world. This master of achievement known as the Roman Empire reigned for over 1,000 years. Our founding fathers applied Solin's and the Roman's principles to The United States constitution. Just as the Roman Empire was, the United States is a representative Republic, which is on the right side of the political spectrum. Our founders chose a representative Republic because it limits the powers of government in our lives to about 15-20%. This is the ideal amount of government control to which we should be subject. America is a great nation because it is a Republic, which means rule of law, not the rule of powerful politicians or charming intellectuals.

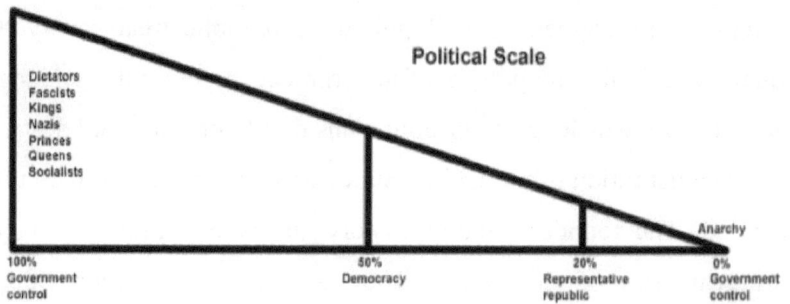

Some Americans think we are a Democracy. We are not a Democracy. See political scale. ☐

In a Democracy, rules change according to majority rule. The word Democracy comes from two Greek words (DEMOS - People) and (KRATEIN - To Rule). Democracy therefore means the rule of the people, or majority rule. This sounds good until one day the majority decides to take away your land, your wealth, or your family! Obviously, there has to be a limit. The major flaw in a Democracy is that the majority isn't held back, and if more than half the people can be persuaded to want something in a Democracy, they get their way! Once more than half the people can be convinced to take away people's wealth, kill a race of people, or enslave another, then those are the new rules and laws. Most of the nation adapts to new way of life without question. With majority rule, anything irrational can and eventually will happen.

In a Republic, we are governed by laws as they are written. The word REPUBLIC comes from the Latin (RES - Thing) and (PUBLICA - Public), meaning "The Public Thing," or THE LAW! A true Republic is one in which the government is limited by LAW, leaving the people alone. Our constitution put a limit on government control and gave freedom to its citizens. This freedom provided by our constitution contributed more benefits to humankind than any other system of government. Unfortunately, like all systems of government, elitist socialist under the cloak of Democracy and fairness infiltrate free nations governments and spread socialism like cancer. The world hasn't changed much in the past few thousand years. It happened in the past to the Roman Empire and it will happen to us unless we stop our government from completely ruling our lives. Government left unchecked is like cancer; they create controlling authorities to regulate our lives. Before we know it, they control every part of our lives. The mayhem of the past shaped our founding fathers' vision to create a system of government that protects its citizens from overbearing government. The constitution clearly states that government shall have limited powers over its citizens' freedoms. You may wonder why we need protection from the federal government. Throughout history, governments have been responsible for murdering their own citizens and restricting people's freedoms all over the world. It happened all throughout history for thousands of years. In recent history, it happened in the old Soviet Union, Cambodia, Burma, and Rwanda, just to name a few. It's happening now in North Korea and some countries in the Middle East. In the past, civilizations fell because governments became intrusive and oppressive. Left unchecked, our government will surely take away all our freedoms and in time enslave us all.

☐☐

For America, the road to liberty was not smooth. Our founding fathers argued relentlessly during the creation of our constitution and the bill of rights. There were insults and unnecessary comments flying back and forth between these brilliant, educated men. They were debating! True debate, not the sideshow we see today on television. Needless to say, even though there was a lot of disagreement, the final results were truly exceptional. The resulting documents survived the test of time and are used as blueprints by nations around the world. These documents have been around longer than any other constitution in the past 1,000 years. Our founders blessed us with a Republic. Most Americans today have no idea what a Republic is, it should be required teaching in schools so no one forgets. It would be a shame to lose our nation to the control of a few socialists because people don't bother to learn about our system of government. ☐

Like in the past, today, we still live under the invisible hand of the federal government, which is wrapped around our throats, tightening its grip every so often. Before America was established, there were kings, czars, and warlords controlling lives and behaviors of people all over the world. Today, governments control us via the Departments of Energy, Agriculture, Education, and 21 other federal departments. Today unqualified leaders who are constantly tampering with every federal department manipulate our lives. Their job is to regulate our behavior and our lives. The federal government is deeply involved in our lives, and most of us don't even realize it. The fact that the government became so large and powerful is dangerous because they have also become corrupt and harmful to citizens. We the people have to put a stop to this or things will only get worse. It's easy to fall into a violent, turbulent society where crime is rampant.

Living in America in the 21st century, most of us have no idea what life was like 200, 500, or 1000 years ago. With all the luxuries and comforts we have today, it would be hard to imagine a day in the life of the average person in the past. There was truly a lot of hardship. Life was filled with manual labor and it was very unsanitary. Whatever people needed, it was not as simple as turning on the faucet or flipping on the light switch. To get light at night, you had to use candles, for heat, you had to get a fire started. Wood was not delivered; someone had to go outside and chop it up. There were no phones, no refrigerators, no televisions, or any other luxuries. The average life expectancy was under 50 years of age for thousands of years before America was founded. Infant mortality rates were over 50%. Some people lived past 50 years of age, but the world did not have as many senior citizens as it does today.

Our founders understood what horrible consequences occur to civilizations when left under the rule of powerful and corrupt individuals. They realized that man, left to his own resources can be more productive with no government looking over his shoulder and deciding what he can and can't do. These lessons learned from history led our founders to write a constitution and a bill of rights that specifically gives NO rights to the federal government over its citizens. President Obama found this troubling and would like to change this. In a 2001 interview, Obama said the following on a radio interview: *"And to the extent as radical I think as people tried to characterize the Warren Court, it wasn't that radical. It didn't break free from the essential constraints that were placed by the Founding Fathers in the Constitution, at least as it's been interpreted. The Warren Court interpreted it in the same way that generally the Constitution is a charter of negative liberties. It says what the states can't do to you. It says what the federal government can't do to you, but it doesn't say what the federal government or the state government must do on your behalf."*

President Obama doesn't like the U. S. constitution the document that gives us all the freedoms we enjoy the way it is. His last 12 words in that interview said it all: *"The federal government or the state government MUST DO on your behalf. "* What if the government says we must do something evil, like condemn one race of people? Or condemn one religion? It happened in Germany, Yugoslavia, the Middle East, and Asian and African nations. This also happened in the past, hundreds of years ago, this is exactly why our founders did not include any reference to what the government can or must do on our behalf.

In the past 200 years, America has prospered, created, innovated, and liberated more than any other nation on earth in a short time of its presence. This all happened because our citizens were free from the oppression of kings, governments, warlords, and other insane powers. We were able to prosper because God is on the side of free people. Needless to say, being separated by oceans from the rest of the world helped keep tyrants at bay and away from America. The truth was out, and people were flocking to America by the hundreds of thousands. People knew back then, as they do now, that in America, they were free to create a vibrant society without the overbearing hand of the government. With all this freedom, citizens utilized their skills and creativity. They prospered beyond their wildest dreams thanks to their newfound freedom. This is how America was able to become a super power in a short time compared to other nations in the world. In the beginning, our politicians in the federal government were busy politicking, lying, cheating, and misleading. Back in the 19th century and part of the 20th century, politicians didn't have the power to hold back innovation and production the way they do today. Our founders understood the death grip that powerful rulers can have over their citizens. They believed that no one person should be different in the eyes of the law. This was a new concept for many, because it had always been held that the rich and elite are judged differently. Thanks to the wisdom of our founders, we all became equal in the eyes of God. There still is a double standard in which the rich are able to circumvent the laws. It happens all over the world today. With some flaws, the American system of justice comes closest to fair and equal law out of any other nation on earth.□

□

Americans are no different from any other people in the world, yet we have excelled at everything. We excelled because our government was not over intrusive and gave people liberty to be what they want to be, in pursuit of happiness. In the beginning, the government didn't have the power to levy taxes on us and punish our achievers as much as they do today. America has spread its wealth, prosperity, and creativity like no other nation on earth. America embraced peaceful nations and created peaceful alliances to spread freedom, wealth and justice all through the world. We are citizens from all over the world with ties to every nation in the world. People come to America from all nations, for a chance at freedom and success. This is the America people around the world got to know as they saw their friends, relatives, and neighbors immigrate to America reap the rewards and riches America has to offer. Sadly, in the last 100 years, our federal government has become dictatorial and expanded like never before, creating new ways to control our lives. Like in the past, the power and corruption overcame greedy politicians who have been creating obstacles to progress for the past 100 years. Currently, the obstacles Congress uses are departments; these are equivalent to dictatorial powers. Our government's reckless behavior via manipulating departments put our nation into severe recessions and cost millions of people's fortunes in the past century. Whether the government is manipulating energy or education or agriculture, Congress now rules our lives the same way kings ruled over their people in the past. In the past, kings, bishops, popes, or dukes decided what science was (Galileo comes to mind). They decided who got to own land, who got to live, what people paid in taxes and tariffs, and people's faith. In contrast, in November 2009, the federal government decided that human-made global warming is real and we should be taxed on carbon emissions. Like in the past, the rulers decide what science is and what it is not.

Life in the past was about the rule of force. The British Empire trekked around the world and colonized and robbed many nations of their treasure and wealth. The Dutch trekked around the world, robbed people of their citizens, and created a slave trade around the world. The French colonized, as did the Spanish and other European nations. Citizens of many of these nations were fed up with their tyrannical kings oppressing freedom of religion. Many ventured to America for freedom from persecution and a chance at a better life. Two hundred years ago, there were many European immigrants who came to America for the same reasons everyone else did freedom from oppression of kings and tyrants. Some brought their customs of slave trading, while others brought their carpentry, blacksmithing, and culinary skills in. Some of these new immigrants came to America and chose to continue the slave trade as they did in their home countries. America accepted slavery with hesitation and deep resentment, and in the north, slavery was frowned upon. Every American president knew it was a matter of time before the slavery issue would be dealt with. When Abraham Lincoln was president, American finally faced up to this dark spot in history and fought a civil war to end slavery and keep America united. After over 600,000 lives were lost, freedom prevailed for all people! This young nation fought a brutal and violent civil war, yet America did not split apart. America stood united during the civil war thanks to our strong foundation, our constitution. It is a testament to just how solid the foundation of our nation is, for even a civil war within couldn't tear us apart. No other nation survived civil wars and stood united when all was over.

After the revolutionary and civil wars, the United States proved itself a formidable power in the world. We showed civility by not colonizing the nations with which we went to war after 1900. America liberated more people than any other nation in history. In the case of the Mexican war, perhaps everyone would have been a lot better off if Mexico had been annexed and had become part of the United States. In WWI, WWWII, the Korean War, the Vietnam War, the Gulf War, and Yugoslavia, the United States liberated, helped set up functioning governments, and rebuilt nations with which it went to war. The amount of good America has done for the world is not matched by any other nation or empire. America sends food and aid all over the world, yet many despise us. We have been an asset and possibly the most positive contribution to the human race to date. America led the operation to free Kuwait in the 1990s in the first Gulf War. We led the peacekeeping mission in Yugoslavia before Europe had the leadership and organization to enter and help their neighbors stop genocide. America fought wars in the name of freedom, truth, and justice. Before America became a super power, wars were fought to dominate and rule by whatever means necessary. America fights wars to liberate the oppressed, feed the hungry, and protect the weak and innocent. Thanks to the omnipresence of the U.S. around the world, nations no longer conquer other nations, except in Africa. In the recent past, Iraq tried to concur Kuwait, but with the leadership of America, the world came together and stopped the murder and bloodshed started by Saddam Hussein's army. Now, our enemies are wiser and know the only way to defeat us is by terror and deception. This deception used by terrorists comes in many forms. It comes in the form of irresponsible leaders accusing our military of wrongdoings! Some in Congress are even making it difficult for our soldiers to protect themselves. Our generals have to wait on politicians to agree to what is needed in the battlefield eerily similar to Vietnam. ☐

☐

In the 1800s and early 1900s, there was a nation in Europe similar to the United States that was also enjoying success similar to what the US was going through. Before WWI, the largest empire in Europe was the Austrian-Hungarian Empire. It consisted of a handful of nations in central Europe, which made up the largest empire at that time. The Hungarian Empire was enjoying innovation, freedom, and prosperity as America was. At that time, America was still developing and coming out of the civil war. It was at the beginning of the industrial revolution, which was about to change the world forever. Unfortunately, the mentality of European nations has not changed much in the past thousand years. The French, the Germans, and the Russians, who were once the ruling empires in Europe, were not very fond of the powerful influence of the Austrian-Hungarian Empire. When WWI broke out in early 1914, thanks to all the treaties nations had with each other, everyone in Europe was dragged into a senseless war causing the death of hundreds of thousands of innocent people. Instead of just letting the two sides resolve it, nations from all over the world were dragged in because of the treaties. After WWI ended, Europe did everything wrong to ensure wars would no longer break out on the continent of Europe. With the Treaty of Versailles, Europeans decided to punish Germany and split up the Austrian-Hungarian Empire. This created an atmosphere in Europe for a powerful leader to step in and take a leadership role and control of the continent. This was the time Mussolini and Fascism came to power, as did Hitler and the National Socialist Party (Nazi) and Lenin and Stalin with the Communist Party. All three of these insane leftwing maniacs were hell bent on ruling Europe. With Austria and Hungary no longer a powerful empire to curb these tyrants, there was no one to stop the spread of evil around Europe, and bloodshed soon followed via WWII. All the warning signs were there, but the European nations didn't take the dangers seriously. Hitler was building his military and was up to no good in Germany seizing land all around

Germany, marching into neighboring countries all over Europe. Stalin and Lenin were mass murdering their educated citizens. Mussolini was creating havoc in Italy. The prime minister of Hungary at that time, Admiral Horthy, attempted to warn the British and the Americans, but both nations had just come out of WWI and were in no mood to get involved in another conflict. Besides, the economy was about to fall apart thanks to the U.S. Congress manipulating banks, tariffs, and taxes and in turn putting America into a Great Depression.

Over and over we go, in and out of recessions. One notable recession was in the early 1980's; this recession was the direct result of the creation of the Department of Energy. Our nation was in such depressed state that unemployment was over 10%, interest rates to buy a home were close to 20%, and the highest tax rate was over 70%. People were sad and depressed. Then, along came Ronald Reagan and the 1980s. He loosened government's death grip on freedom and released the free will of honest American people. No wonder the 1980s was such a jubilant and exciting decade; we were just released from government tyranny. Now, government is back to where it was in the late 1970s, and it is time for us to make a stand, because dangerous leaders are preparing to ruin our lives just like they did in the past.

Today, there are dozens of people just as ruthless and evil as Hitler, Stalin, and Mussolini of the past. Some of today's evil leaders came to power the same way as the powerful in the past. Insane rulers like Muammar Gaddafi, Hugo Chavez, Fidel Castro, and Kim Jong-Ill, to name a few, are oppressing and enslaving their citizens. These people either were handed power down the family line or lied, cheated, tortured, murdered, and intimidated to get power. They rule with the same mentality of prehistoric barbarians who limit their citizens' freedoms. People unfortunate enough to live under dictators are robbed of opportunities in life. They are trapped and forced to live a life with limited freedoms and possibilities. These dictators rob people of their natural talents because life no longer becomes about individuals; life revolves around the state and the leader. For the past 100 years, our federal government has slowly suffocated the vibrant capitalist spirit out of our nation as well. By creating federal departments, our federal government has overstepped its boundaries and reached into our lives like communists and dictators reach into their citizens' lives. From one central location, powerful politicians control the lives of millions, as kings did in the past. We must contact our representatives and demand that all these departments be closed as soon as possible! We must act now before the U.S.A. becomes U.S.S.A. (United Socialist States of America)! □ Each and every department below takes a piece of our freedom. Tell Congress to close these controlling authorities and stop interfering with our lives.

Committee on Agriculture

Committee on Appropriations

Committee on Armed Services

Committee on the Budget

Committee on Education and Labor

Committee on Energy and Commerce

Committee on Financial Services

Committee on Foreign Affairs

Committee on Homeland Security

Committee on House Administration

Committee on the Judiciary

Committee on Natural Resources

Committee on Oversight and Government Reform

Committee on Rules

Committee on Science and Technology

Committee on Small Business

Committee on Standards of Official Conduct

Committee on Transportation and Infrastructure

Committee on Veterans' Affairs

Committee on Ways and Means

Joint Economic Committee

Joint Congressional Committee on Inaugural Ceremonies

Joint Committee on Taxation

House Permanent Select Committee on Intelligence

House Select Committee on Energy Independence and Global Warming

Visit www.destructivepolitics.com and send an email to Congress demanding they close the federal departments starting with the Department of Energy.

Chapter 6 – Media

"If you believe everything you see on TV, in time, you will wake up to a rude reality."

Reporters in Washington should be fired for incompetence; right under their noses, our federal government has stolen $13 trillion from taxpayers. Our media has not even asked the government where the money is or how they dare consider any new government programs if they are so in debt and irresponsible! From the Sunday talk shows to the nightly news on MSNBC, ABC, CBS, and CNN, every reporter should lose his or her job for standing by while the federal government ran up a $13 trillion debt and almost bankrupted our nation!☐

☐

We read about it all the time; we hear all kinds of news, often not knowing what to believe. Today, we don't have to believe everything that ABC, NBC, CBS CNN, MSNBC, FOX, BLOOMBERG, or the ASSOCIATED PRESS have to say. With the exception of FOX news, the mainstream media have opinion makers pushing certain ideologies. If you don't believe this, you can make the connection by connecting all the dots to the Democrat party and the mainstream media. You will find that people who used to work for the media now work for the White House. During the Clinton administration, some in the media had spouses working in the White House. This completely blurs the line between government and media. The reason FOX is fairer is that they have an overwhelming number of Democrat strategists who are free to speak their minds. ABC, NBC, MSNBC, CNN, and CBS don't have this much input from as many different people's perspectives.

□□

The key to finding true and quality information is doing quality research. The best source of quality information is right at our fingertips on the Internet. If we were to rely on the mainstream media for information, we would be mislead and only shown what they want us to see. The mainstream media is the SYSTEM; it is the enemy within, and it is no longer serving the public. The mainstream media now serves our federal government, and they collaborate with government officials on how to best get their ideas across to taxpayers. It is not the media itself, but the current batch of reporters and anchors running the mainstream news organizations. They are mostly liberal Democrats who believe in the socialist ideas of the Democratic Party. They don't question any of the catastrophic failures, which are departments the federal government runs. They also don't question the $13 trillion national debt run up by Congress and lying politicians. Some in the media have regular meetings with the White House communications office to discuss how they will present the news and the message the White House wants to convey to the American people. These meetings between the White House and the mainstream media happen on a regular basis and do not seem to bother anyone.

In the summer of 2009, ABC offered itself up for a two-hour long infomercial by president Obama to sell the Universal Government Controlled Insurance Reform Health Care Bill. The entire network including NBC sold its soul to the United States Government and became the media branch of the federal government. Now the government uses our media as their bully pulpit. The news anchors are intertwined with the federal government, and the media no longer challenge our politicians. Instead, our reporters are more like stenographers and just take notes. The sad truth is, the following five important items should be dealt with by the government, but the press is not asking any questions of them about these issues, nor is the press reporting on the fraud and abuse in government:

1. *Medicare has over $40 billion in annual corruption*
2. *Federal government caused the market and mortgage collapse*
3. *Government healthcare reform will kill us in our golden years*
4. *Our Energy Department is hurting our economy*
5. *Speaker Pelosi is corrupt and covers up Democrat corruption*

Why has the press not looked deeper into these five very important issues? Are they not aware of the Medicare corruption? Do they not care about complaints from nations with universal healthcare? Why won't our media investigate and report on the news that universal health care will ration medicine for the old and the poor? The quality of universal healthcare will drop and the senior citizen mortality rate will rise if congress gets this bill passed.

All this information is readily available, yet the mainstream news media is not talking about this. Why do they not investigate the Energy Department and see how many politicians are tied to alternative energy? If our media were really doing their jobs, universal healthcare and alternative energy would not be debated in Congress. The reform we would be discussing would be tort reform, eliminating federal mandates and insurance competition across state lines. With the media on the federal government's side, instead of asking challenging questions from the government, ABC, NBC, and CBS are pushing the government programs and actually challenging citizens and doctors on why we should have universal healthcare. Yes, the media is not investigating what the federal government officials are doing; they choose to investigate private companies and citizens instead. Meanwhile, the Democrats use Freddie Mac and Fannie Mae as piggybanks and mismanaged them to the brink of bankruptcy.

The corruption and deceit goes deep, the people who are getting jobs in the government and the White House are not concerned about the constitution or our rights. They are concerned about power, control, and pushing an ideology onto unsuspecting Americans. Some of these people finding new employment in the White House used to be reporters who were covering the campaign and writing unbiased news articles about their future boss Barack Obama. Keep in mind, media is supposed to be unbiased; our media is not! They routinely comingle, befriend, and interact with the politicians and the White House; this compromises the media's ability to remain unbiased. Every one of the CBS, NBC, ABC,

CNN, and MSNBC reporters should be removed and replaced with people who have no affiliation with anyone in the government. The problem with the media is they are friends with people in the government.

So how has the media betrayed us? In modern times, we can look back to the 1970s when Richard Nixon was fighting the Vietnam War. Our press was already attacking and hurting our soldiers and creating a dangerous atmosphere here in the U.S. While our brave military was fighting the ultimate battle against the evil soviet communist empire from expanding, the American press was busy labeling our soldiers "baby killers" and "murderers." They conveniently neglected the mass murders that the Soviet Empire was perpetrating against nations all over the World. As usual, the press portrayed horrific news and images, doing all they could to destroy the spirit of the United States military. They forgot to mention the horrors of communists and dictators were committing and how they started the Vietnam War. Instead of supporting and encouraging the fight against evil communists, our media was turning millions of Americans at home against our own soldiers who were risking life and limb in Vietnam. When Walter Cronkite announced, *"the war is lost,"* President Johnson responded, *"If I have lost Walter Cronkite, I've lost America."* Johnson was misled and fell for Cronkite's half-baked report. Instead of listening to TV and getting 2nd or 3rd hand information, Johnson should have discussed it with his generals. Thanks to our media's dereliction of duty and meddling in international affairs, over 35,000 brave American servicemen lost their lives for an unaccomplished mission. The media and the U.S. Congress destroyed the spirit and will of the American soldier in Vietnam the same way they are doing now in Afghanistan.

The media doesn't seem to care what evil and atrocities communists, dictators and terrorists have committed. They don't scrutinize congress much unless someone in congress is standing up for the accomplishments of our troops. Instead, some in the Main Stream media attack our military and often blow things way out of proportion. They accuse our soldiers of torture and abuse of prisoners in Guantanamo Bay Cuba. Prisoners who stay in Guantanamo Bay stay an average of 14 months, during this period; they leave about 12 lbs heavier than when they arrived. It seems lately our media has always been on the wrong side. When Reagan was running against Jimmy Carter, the media was attacking Reagan as old, simple-minded, and clueless. The media elites were certain Reagan was going to destroy the economy the economy Jimmy Carter, the genius with a 156 IQ, wrecked in his short and painful four-year term. In his book on Reagan, Dinesh D'Souza wrote about how Reagan was greeted by the Washington elite establishment. Everything Reagan sought to accomplish seemed ludicrous and uneducated to the long-standing liberals. The elite liberals thought tax cuts would create uncontrollable inflation. A foreign policy based on the extreme notion that communism should be put on the ash heap of history was dismissed as a belligerent fantasy too dangerous for the nuclear age. At the end of his term, Reagan was the wise man, and all his opponents Democrats and RINO Republicans, political scientist and economists, "Sovietologists" and journalists were proven to be the ignorant dummies. Throughout the 1980s, the media was constantly attacking Reagan as a senile, old man who needed to take naps; he was against the poor and for the rich. This was the media template, and it was nonstop. When Reagan appointed Clarence Thomas to the Supreme Court of the United States, the media created a false story and ran with it on every paper, trying to disqualify a black American from becoming a Supreme Court judge. The mainstream media has sided with the socialist liberal Democrats and has been assisting Democrats in slowly taking away our freedoms and branding honest men as corrupt public servants. When the press starts to befriend politicians, the ones who get hurt are the citizens who depend on the press for unbiased, accurate news. Accurate reporting is the path to informed citizens voting for qualified candidates.

☐

The mainstream media doesn't hold back. When George H. Bush was running for office, the press, again with the help of the Democrats, tried to do their best to get a Democrat in the White House. At that time, it was Governor Dukakis from Massachusetts. The press did all they could to keep George H. Bush from winning. Fortunately for George H. Bush, the Reagan legacy was still intact, and he was able to win due largely to the large part of the nation whose hearts Ronald Reagan had won. This helped George H. Bush for his first term, but in the second term, he had no chance. Again, with the assistance of the press, the Democratic Congress put George H. Bush in a position where he was forced to raise taxes. This didn't help him when he was running for his second term against Bill Clinton. The press was naturally brutal to G.H. Bush and was doing all it could to cover up and not report Bill Clinton's shady, corrupt past. It didn't help G.H. Bush that Ross Perot ran as a third party candidate for president. Perot's candidacy largely contributed to G.H. Bush's loss. The fact is that the media was blatantly lying to Americans, saying we were in a deep recession when we were not in a deep recession and lying about the true state of the economy.

Once Clinton entered the White House, the press was on full alert. They were responsible for ensuring that whatever negative news turned up about Clinton, will be presented to limit its impact as much as possible. Clinton had all kinds of baggage following him from Arkansas. He had a long-term extramarital affair. He was repeatedly misusing and abusing his powers as governor. There was corruption a mile long, but that did not seem to matter to our liberal press since they just got one of their guys in there. Needless to say, the problems were just about to begin. On February 26, 1993, terrorists bombed the World Trade Center (WTC). Instead of finding where they were training more terrorists and dropping a bigger bomb on them, Clinton decided to take them to court. The Main Stream Media was on board with Clinton and saw no need to take it any further than the U.S. district courts in New York City. Looking back, Clinton should have sent in the military and carpet-bombed the terrorists training for future terror in the Middle East.

Naturally, the press does not feel Clinton did anything wrong by not taking the first WTC attack seriously. This was not just any president in the White House; this was Bill Clinton, a good friend of the Main Stream Media. The media held back and covered a lot of shady activities and unethical behavior by the Clintons. Any Republican president would have been impeached and thrown in jail had they done half the things Clinton had done. The press was not concerned about Clinton or his ways. From the day the White House requested a 30-day delay on drug tests for White House cabinet members to the sequentially numbered money orders received by the Clinton campaign fund, the press was not concerned with what the Clintons were up to or who was giving them money for reelection. The biggest story the press tried to sit on (but was unsuccessful because it was just too big to hold back) was the Monica Lewinsky affair. The press was sitting on the story and a brave reporter leaked the story to the Drudge Report. That is when the news about Clinton's sex scandal with Miss Lewinsky came to the public's attention. Monica Lewinsky was an intern who was just three years older than Clinton's own daughter, Chelsea. While the Clintons were working and residing in the White House, President Clinton was often preoccupied with cabinet members and interns. The mainstream media was beside itself trying to find a way to explain this to the American people without Clinton getting impeached. They sent out all the talking heads to convince America that what Clinton did was just sex and everyone does it. The truth is, we can write a 500-page book on all the Clinton scandals and abuses of power. The mainstream media treats Democrats differently than Conservative Republicans. During Bill Clinton's campaign for his second term, there was a poll taken of the media. It turned out that over 80% of our media elites voted for Bill Clinton.

It makes one wonder if these reporters were writing unbiased news articles.

After Clinton's term was up and he left the White House, Al Gore naturally stood up to try to take his place in office. He ran against George W. Bush from Texas. As soon as Bush became a serious contender, the press became unrelenting and attacked President Bush until he left office in 2008. Before G.W. Bush became president, the lies and accusations about him started flying from every direction. He was accused of being born with a silver spoon in his mouth. They argued that because of his father, he was getting special treatment throughout his life and in the military draft. Meanwhile, Al Gore, who really did get preferential treatment while growing up, was never criticized or chastised in the media. All kinds of lies and rumors were written about G.W. Bush, but fortunately, none seemed to hurt his chances of becoming president. The mainstream media opposed G.W. Bush with a passion. They did not want to see him win, that is why they started rumors that Bush stole the election from Al Gore in Florida 2001. That is simply not true! Every major newspapers, TV stations, judges, lawyers, and activists were down in Florida counting votes three times! It was undeniable that George W. Bush won the election fair and square. Even this undeniable truth did not change the opinion of the mainstream media. Even today, some still go on TV and claim that George W. Bush stole the election from Al Gore.

If you were alive and conscious from 2000 to 2008, then you know that the press has been attacking G.W. Bush and blaming everything in the world on Bush. Most people do not know or don't care, but Bush inherited a recession from Clinton. The media never mentions this, because they want Clinton to have a good legacy. As soon as he took office, Bush wanted to cut taxes and give Americans a break. What started out as an $800 billion tax cut in the House dwindled down to just over $400 billion in tax cuts. President Bush's tax cuts were fought tooth and nail by lawyers, Democrats, and the press. Imagine that the President wanted to put more money in taxpayers' pockets and the press, with the help of Democrats and a pack of lawyers, opposed it. President Bush wanted to put money in our pocket and some how he became a bad president. If you search online, you will find it is nearly impossible to find a positive story on G.W. Bush even thought he has done so much good for this world, yet our media and Democrats couldn't care less.

The Main Stream Media constantly accused Bush and Cheney of manipulating intelligence and misleading us into war. The press purposely did not mention that G.W. Bush acted on the same intelligence that Bill Clinton saw. The press also left out that members of the House Intelligence Committee also witnessed the same exact intelligence that Bush and Cheney witnessed. All these facts are omitted from most stories because it vindicates Bush and Cheney. It also proves that the Democrats and the press knew everything and voted yes on the same bills that Bush signed. After 911, Bush organized a coalition to go in and get Al Qaeda in Afghanistan. Surprisingly, the press did not give him too much resistance over this, most likely because of the 9/12 mindset. Everyone in America was upset and wanted to see us strike back hard! With Congress, the Senate, intelligence, and America on board, and the coalition of over a dozen nations, we went into Afghanistan in 2001.

After the war wound down in Afghanistan, the media started attacking Bush again. This time, President Bush decided we should take preemptive action to prevent future terror attacks and wars in America. He went to the United Nations and demanded that they start enforcing their sanctions and punishing nations that broke the rules set forth by a group of nations. Iraq has broken over 150 sanctions, from human rights to selling oil for arms, yet the UN sanctions (sanctions are supposed to be punishments) did absolutely nothing. That is like a mob boss in America killing, looting, stealing, and taking whatever he wants because he knows that the police will just issue him another citation. President George W. Bush went to the UN and informed them that if they didn't do something about Iraq, America will. George Bush waited one year and had Congress vote on two resolutions of war before we attacked Iraq and got rid of Saddam Hussein! Saddam Hussein was a true terrorist thug who among other things employed a rapist in his army of thugs and murders. Had the mainstream press done their job, they would have discovered that Saddam Hussein removed many weapons of mass destructions from Iraq during the one-year debate to the run up to the war in.

With the leadership of George W. Bush, America and the coalition liberated over 50 million Muslims from the tyranny of terrorists and evil warlords. Instead of the press acknowledging this, they looked for any excuse to criticize George W. Bush and an excuse to try Bush or Cheney in World Court for war crimes. It came to a point where if anything went wrong in the world, it was G.W. Bush's fault. The media did all they could to paint Bush as incompetent, way over his head, and involved in too much conflict. They did everything they could to make Bush sound horrible, including counting bodies as they were coming back from Iraq. The mainstream media was eagerly awaiting the 3,000 Death Toll in Iraq so they could blame G.W. Bush for the loss of innocent lives. These soldiers did not fall in vain! Their brave acts of heroism saved millions of Americans as well as freed millions of oppressed people around the world. The Iraqi liberation movement was one of the most successful wars fought in history. When it comes to length of war and casualties of war, there are few wars that have been as successful with minimal damage done. The military's number one objective is minimal casualties in any conflict. This is more important now than ever before.

During WWII, in just one training exercise America suffered a horrible loss of over 800 brave servicemen in a single day. This is not to say that the 4,000 lives lost in Afghanistan/Iraq are not much compared to the lives lost in other wars, this is to show that we are fighting wars more cautiously with more emphasis and the safety of our brave military.

Civil War over 600,000 deaths
WWI over 100,000 deaths
WWII over 400,000 deaths
Korean War over 35,000 deaths

Vietnam War over 50,000 deaths
Gulf War I over 2,000, deaths
Iraq and Afghanistan War on terror over 4,000 deaths

War is horrible and causes a lot of hurt among many of us. When asking if it is worth going to war, all we have to ask ourselves is whether we want to wait for extremists to come and attack us like in the 1993 WTC bombing or the 911 terrorist attack. The clear and present danger does not allow us to stand back and let evil spread around the world without check. Oceans can no longer protect us from evil. If we do not stop them from killing in their own country and raising suicide mass murderers, terrorists will soon come to our country to kill us too. They did it in 1993 and in 2001, and they have been trying to do it each and every year, but our nation's intelligence has been able to prevent terror attacks in the U.S. since 2001. The media must stay on top of this story and investigate the terrorists the way they investigated Sarah Palin. It is most important that we stay on offense with terrorists, or we will be attacked again.

The press has been ignoring what's important in the world. They don't focus enough attention on the roots of terror or how we can put a stop new terror seeds from being planted. It's obvious by the sates of our world that powerful media and politicians are mismanaging our lives. The Health Care Bill, Cap and Trade, bank Bail Outs are important issues about which the press has not been upfront or have been ignoring. These things are all vital to our survival; inexpensive energy, affordable healthcare and fair just banking system are as important to us as the air we breathe.

When you read the constitution, you will not find any mention of healthcare, climate change, the IRS, Social Security, Medicare, education, or energy. It's just not there! Yet, our government decided it is in their interest to create these departments and to control them, of all of them. The American media should be investigating and questioning the destructive nature of all the departments the federal government has created in the past 100 years. Our federal government has completely wrecked everything, and they are blaming taxpayers for it. Where is our honest media? Why is the mainstream press not pointing out the truth about who and what caused the problems we face today? The federal government destroyed just about everything from taxes to retirement to healthcare. They are stealing trillions of dollars and telling us they will fix health care while Medicare has over $60 billion fraud. All governments ever say is "we are going to fix it by creating a new department, new regulations" and what do you get in the end? Higher taxes, bankrupt social security, Medicare filled with fraud, and national debt over $13 trillion. So where is the media scrutiny over all this corruption? Why are they not asking the questions about what happened to the social security money and why Medicare is filled with so much fraud and corruption? The press is busy hiding negative stories in the back pages of newspapers; they are ignoring relevant facts about government programs, budgets, and our president's reckless behavior. The press is a big reason for our problems. They are completely ignoring our $13 trillion national debt. They are attacking private citizens and blaming "greedy" corporations on the problems of the world today.

Instead, they should focus on international terror, job loss, the state of economy, and corruption in Congress by greedy politicians.

It's not difficult to realize the damage done by the federal government, yet where is our mainstream media? The Department of Commerce is hurting businesses across the nation, Medicare has corruption costing tens of billions annually, and Medicaid and Social Security are bankrupt! With the power of the mainstream media, we should be knocking down the doors of Congress demanding that they close down every department they have created, audit them and then shut them down. These departments are destroying our lives, our nation, our families, and our jobs.

In the past 100 years, the federal government has started to put up obstacles and barriers to keep us from pursuing quality and prosperous lives. They hurt us with every Federal they have created and the mainstream press has done nothing to point out the disaster in the making. One damaging department is the Department of Education; this department removed standards and slowly started phasing out competitiveness from public schools. Due to federal government involvement, dropout rates are on the rise in inner city public schools, as is illiteracy. Where is the money? We have spent over 1 Trillion dollars with nothing to show for it. Where is our mainstream press investigating this fraud?

Thanks to the federal Department of Energy, we are paying as much as three times the cost of energy if the Energy Department did not exist. Why is the press not investigating this? The very department that is supposed to ensure that federal taxes from gasoline sales are used to repair roads and bridges is the department used as a political tool and piggybank by Democrats to spend money for pet social projects. Where is the press investigating? Thanks to the Energy Department, Congress ensured that we must depend on foreign countries for oil some of which countries are not friendly to the United States. Why is our press not pointing this out? This is more of a reason to drill for our own oil in the United States and stop buying oil from terror sponsoring states. Some of the nations we buy oil from use money from oil sale to buy weapons and create havoc around the world. This enrichment of these rogue nations is causing a lot of instability around the world, all because Democrats will not allow us to drill for our own oil here in America and create jobs.

Thanks to our mainstream media and the Democratic Party, we are now at the mercy of foreign dictators and leaders who truly hate the US! Yes, we are buying oil and enriching nations, which are nuking up and planning to send our money back to us in the form of a big bomb eventually attacking the United States. They will not declare war they will just attack us, and then declare war. Countries like Venezuela and Iran are both oil-rich countries, which sell their oil to the world market. It is not only the U.S.A, Europe and Asia are also buying oil from nations run by evil dictators. Because the Democratic Party purposely wants to control the flow of energy and keep America down, we are arming these dangerous evil nations at the same time Congress and President are ensuring us that the evil threats are no longer as dangerous as before. The press is either clueless or they want to control. If mainstream media were concerned about you and your family, they would attack Congress and demand they drill for oil in America (off the coast of Alaska, Florida, California, and Texas). They would also demand the building of nuclear power plants. So why are they not telling Congress to act now and bring us affordable energy? Where is the media? The media is probably attacking some republican for calling a terrorist a terrorist. Repeatedly, the Main Stream Media is ignoring the harm terrorist have done, the problem with universal health care, the US national debt clock which is the proof of all the corruption and lies in that goes on in Washington D.C. Will the media ever get it?

Congress already stole all our social security money. There is nothing there; it's gone. The Democrats have been lying to us, and they purposely destroyed the financial markets to make Bush look like a bad president. While this was happening, where was the mainstream media? They were most likely attacking Bush for going to war against mass-murdering terrorists. During the war, Democrats did all they could to block social security reform five years ago. The press did nothing to stop the Democrats. Congress basically said to America: *"We are going to hold your retirement money and you can't do anything about it."* That is exactly what they did this is why Social Security was not reformed. All Bush wanted to do was privatize a small portion of it so greedy politicians couldn't put their hands on it. The press, being the watchdogs for the people, did not seem interested in this and attacked Bush for the war instead.

It would have been safe in the market if the Democrats did their civic duties in the Senate and ensured the security of Fannie Mae and Freddie Mac. Now, we find they lied, cheated, and forced banks to lend out money to anyone with a pulse and an I.D., any kind of I.D.; they didn't care. The mainstream media didn't seem bothered by any of the corruption happening right under their noses. Banks started meeting the new government requirements and often lent up to 120% of the value of homes. Where was the mainstream media? Probably writing a story about the American military killing innocent Muslims! The press and Congress are truly shameless.

If our press were truly doing their jobs, Rep. Barney Frank and Senator Chris Dodd would be in front of a judiciary committee answering questions. Why is Nancy Pelosi not bought up on charges for willful negligence or treason for accusing the CIA of misleading Congress? Why does the press shut up when a Democrat tells them to?

This just proves the corrupt nature of our federal government. It also shows the media has become flawed, but only temporarily. Now it's up to the citizens to get the truth out and take back powers that belong to the people, not to Nancy Pelosi, Barack Obama, or Harry Reid. What does Nancy Pelosi know about education? Energy? Healthcare? Does she have any idea what it takes to become a doctor? Open a clinic? Pay for all the equipment, employees, facilities, taxes, loans and all the rules and regulations crammed down their necks by Congress? No, she does not know, nor does she care, and it goes the same for the rest of our elected officials. The fact is that these people have failed at everything in government, with the exception of getting elected. Why is our press not pointing out the inexperience, the lack of qualifications, or the destructive nature of these politicians? Why do the press not ask Department Heads what qualifies them to control the Department they are chairing?

The problem with our mainstream press is the Democrats found a way to manipulate them and own them via tarp bailout money. With the press on their side, the Democrats are attempting to ensure a permanent majority by way of lying, cheating, and stealing more seats in the House and Senate. You can trace this back to the 1990s, or even earlier. In the mid-1990s, Newt Gingrich became Speaker of The House of Representatives and took Congress back from socialists. His first initiative was Pass The Contract with America! This was also the time the House Banking Scandal broke out. Back in the early 1990s, the Democrats were so corrupt that some Congressmen stole over $100,000 dollars and even went to jail for it. After that debacle, Democrats made sure they would not go to jail for stealing money anymore. They figured new and creative ways to steal money and circumvent the laws. That is what lawyers in Washington D.C. are good at finding loopholes and stealing money. Instead of focusing on corrupt Democrats, the press decided to focus on Gingrich instead.

The long, dreaded half-century tyrannical rule by the Democratic Party has cost the American people millions of lives, lost opportunities, and wasted trillions of dollars on failed programs. The federal government has been trying to fix welfare and lift people out of poverty for over 100 years. Each time, they have managed to put more people into poverty and create a hopeless future for millions. Where is the press pointing out this colossal failure? There is no end in sight to the amount of spending that is going on in Washington, D.C. Budgets no longer mean anything; they are just for show. Bills don't mean anything; they get signed so there can be a signing ceremony and the press can take their pictures. The people who are supposed to oversee the system are standing by as politicians drive our nations deeper into debt and destruction.   □□

When Newt Gingrich took over Congress in 1994, the first order of business was called The Contract with America. Basically, it was a set of rules that Congress would have to live by the democrats strongly opposed these changes and found ways to circumvent each one of them:

1- Require all laws that apply to the rest of the country also apply equally to the Congress;

2- select an independent auditing firm to conduct an audit of Congress for waste, fraud or abuse;

3- cut the number of House committees, and cut committee staff by one-third;

4- limit the terms of all committee chairs;

5- ban the casting of proxy votes in committee;

6- require committee meetings to be open to the public;

7- require a three-fifths majority vote to pass a tax increase;

8- guarantee honest accounting of the federal budget with zero base line budgeting.

These are basic, straightforward rules that make sense and would protected the taxpayers. The Democrats oppose and break most of these rules on a regular basis. The press doesn't care; they see it, glance over it and focus on a sex scandal or a housewife from Alaska. Not only that, when the press reports on Democrats, no matter how bad the incident, they try to make it look as if what they do is not a big deal. Often the press will purposely avoid doing an important story on a Democrat if it makes the Democrat look bad. As you read news stories about a Congressman or woman who has done something wrong, you will notice that the party affiliation hardly gets mentioned if it's a Democrat. At the same time, when a Republican does something wrong, his party affiliation is plastered all over the paper and the mainstream news makes sure they mention his party affiliation at least a dozen times in a half-hour show. A perfect example is Democratic Congressman William Jefferson of Louisiana. He was found with $100,000 cash in his freezer. The mainstream media reported on this story, conveniently leaving out the party affiliation. They hardly made a big deal about this corrupt politician.

Until the mainstream media begins pointing the finger at Congress and the federal government for our problems, nothing will change for the better. As time goes on, things will continue to deteriorate steadily until a breaking point. This is damaging our trust in government and the mainstream media. This is also why alternative media is becoming such an important part of our lives today. Americans who follows what is going on in Washington have become aware that our mainstream media cannot be trusted for honest and accurate news. They have simply become the bully pulpit of the federal government. When our national media gives a second take to a Democratic presidential nominee like John Kerry because he got the first question wrong or he said it wrong, it really tells us just whose side the media is really on. It's definitely not the people!

We must take back the media and let people know the truth. email to the mainstream media and congress; let them know you don't appreciate their collaboration and demand that the Department of Energy is shut down!

==========================

Chapter 7 – Taxes

==========================

"How does the government expect us to spread our wealth around when they are taking our wealth away?"

T ax cuts really work! Yes, it is undeniable; every time this nation experienced growth and prosperity, it always occurred when taxes were low and government was not over-intrusive in our lives. On the other hand, every time we had a recession, depression or economic slow down, it was due to higher taxes, more federal rules and regulations. Government is raising our taxes and regulating energy like never before. Weather its through the IRS or the Department of Energy or the EPA, our cost of living is constantly manipulated and tampered with. The federal government creates laws and new regulations to put more control in the hands of a few in Washington D.C.

In the summer of 2009, with the leadership of Nancy Pelosi, Congress passed a new energy bill called The Cap and Trade Bill. If it makes it through the Senate, this bill will increase regulations, fees and penalties on businesses involved with the mining and production of energy and everyday products. It will increase the cost of living for every single American who uses energy. From gasoline, electricity, and heating oil to public transportation, buses, trains, airplanes, boats, trucks, you name it the prices will rise if cap and trade becomes law. Most Americans have no idea what's in store for them, and they don't care until it happens just like in the summer of 2008 when the average price of gasoline was $4.85/gallon. People started to care and get upset when the price of energy shot up and it was affecting their wallets. The same thing will happen with this cap and trade energy bill. We will start to care once the bill directly affects us and we feel the pinch in our wallets.

By passing the punishing cap and trade tax, Congress will increase the cost of energy for every single American, from rich to poor. When we see the energy prices rise, again we will likely see politicians come out and attack businesses for being greedy and raising prices on consumers. As with everything else, we can thank the federal government for the rise in the cost of our basic every day needs: food, fuel, taxes electricity and more. All this happens when the cost of fuel increases, the fuel Tax is the only tax can escape, except for congress.

History clearly shows the damage our federal government has done and is still doing by constantly tampering with our tax code. From the Great Depression to every recession following the great Depression, all can be traced back to one federal department or group of powerful politicians in the federal government creating laws, regulations and eventually problems in peoples lives. How many millions of lives have they ruined? We will never know for sure. On top of government manipulation of our lives via departments, congress is constantly complicating our tax system, making it nearly impossible to confidently fill out taxes without the aid of an accountant. Almost every year, the government finds another way to complicate our tax laws even further. As it is today, our federal tax code is too complex for anyone out side of accountants to decipher.

There is only one effective way to fix our IRS, is to force everyone in Congress and the US Senate to prepare their own taxes, just like they force us to prepare our taxes by April 15th. If our leaders fail to fill out their tax forms correctly, they should be kicked out of Congress and prosecuted by the IRS for fraud, or they can abolish the tax code and simplify it so none of us will have to worry about the IRS ever again! We need to send a message to Congress and the Senate demanding this law! If we can make government do this, we can have a simplified tax bill passed within a short period of time.

People in government don't live under the same rules average American's do; they live above the law and circumvent whatever laws get in their way. Congress doesn't care who they hurt by attacking private companies, nor do they care how many people lose private sector jobs. Our leaders cheat on taxes, cover up corruption and demand that we the citizens pay higher fees and taxes. Every job lost, every home in foreclosure, every savings account emptied can be traced back to problems created by the federal government and their manipulation of our tax laws and energy supplies. Many still blame the Banks, Banks didn't force anyone to take out a loan. Banks do what banks do they lend money to make more money. In our mortgage melt down, banks did what Congress forced them to do ever since 1977 with the Community Reinvestment Act (under this act, lending institutions had to lend money in low income neighborhoods). Congress forced banks to lend money to people who couldn't pay it back! These were good intentions which created big problems down the line, but not because people did not want to pay their bills. People had new homes, good jobs and a chance at living the American Dream. They wanted this to last. As time went on, the leadership changed and the new leaders decided that taxes should be raised and we should be using more bio fuels made from corn. This in turn drove the price of food and energy higher costing everyone including the poor more money. This is how the government hurt the poor. They first show them the path to owning a home, which is honorable and just, but then they turn around and destroy the poor and the middle class by causing the price of our most important commodity (energy) to rise. Higher price of energy is a form of an energy tax. It takes money out of every person's pockets giving us less disposable incomes. Expensive energy guarantees job loss, home foreclosures, businesses and factories closing among other things. High price of energy does not discriminate, nor can you hide from it or cheat it. If you need oil, gas or electricity, you must pay what the market price is.

What does the U.S. government do to stop fraud, abuse, and wasteful spending? ABSOLUTELY NOTHING! Their solution is more government oversight and intervention in private markets. If Congress were under the same scrutiny as the private sector, all departments would be shut down and many representatives would be in jail. As the government piles a heavy burden of taxes and more regulations on small businesses and taxpayers, unemployment keeps rising and people's lives are becoming devastated. Millions of Americans lost homes, life savings, jobs and much more because of the abusive federal government and their unfair complex tax code. This tax code costs taxpayers over $500 billion a year in lost income, time and costs of preparation. The time lost to prepare all the documents and the amount of labor spent on preparing taxes from the time spent filling out to the time spent processing. Included in this $500 billion are the people incarcerated for cheating on taxes and the cost associated with legal fees, persecution, prisons, and much more. If all this money were diverted to medicine or paying off the debt, we would not have to worry about taxes ruling our way of life. Who doesn't stress out on April 15?

Our federal government uses its power to manipulate our tax code on a regular basis. The government's opinion on taxes is when the economy slows then it is time to raise taxes and print trillions of new dollars. Along with higher taxes, they hand out money to unions and organizations, which helped greedy politicians get elected. Our tax dollars are funding corrupt organizations, which helped politicians cheat our election system. No matter how many people disapprove of Congress, currently in 2010(approximately 12%) The Democratic Party does not care and is not willing to reform government spending or our complex tax code. They keep interfering with business and private sector and spending more and more tax dollars. They believe that cutting taxes is what creates deficits. That is completely false! They vote yes on new departments and they always show up for the vote to give themselves a pay raise. There is never a vote to cut pay! People often forget this, but our federal government ran up a $13 trillion debt! We have to pay for that! However, they don't care; they just keep increasing the amount of their credit line by voting on it. This is proof that our entire Congress is corrupt, that they should be stripped of their powers, and that all departments must be shut down or audited then shut down!

Every single federal department is broken, mismanaged, and costing us trillions of dollars a year. Federal departments are also making things extremely difficult for businesses and people to survive. We are paying more for everything because of the departments they have created yet these departments have no benefits. They are all riddled with powerful corrupt politicians who use the departments as fund raising tools and to manipulate the economy. It is simply maddening that our tax dollars are keeping departments open, these departments costing us thousands of jobs and tax dollars every year. If we could eliminate all departments, the government could free up trillions of tax dollars and put it back in the private sector and shore up Medicare and Social Security. They would also have money to pay off the national debt and not just the interest. Closing all federal departments is like loosening a tight noose around our necks. As we remove these departments one by one, we will create an atmosphere that will solve every problem of the world today from world hunger, world peace, and world environment issues to anything else we can imagine. That is the power of tax cuts! That is the power of a free nation.

You don't have to be a rocket scientist or college-educated to understand that when taxes are cut, we all enjoy years of prosperity. Government collected record tax revenues due to the Bush Tax cuts. The economy was growing at a healthy pace and tax income to government was at record levels due to full employment. This happened because when taxes are low, more people work, earning money, and paying taxes. At the same time, more people have disposable incomes to start businesses and hire graduates, people looking for jobs, immigrants, and anyone else that is looking for employment. People living in local communities will have disposable income to hire teenagers to do work around the house for money, this will teach them how to earn and save money. When Taxes are low, people have more money to hire handymen, or anyone looking for work. The power of tax cuts is unmatched by any federal government stimulus to our economy. When taxes are low, wealth spreads at a rate that is incomprehensible. The amazing thing is when taxes are cut in the US; wealth spreads to almost every corner of the world, not just America! When Americans travel, the world prospers and people are lifted out of poverty, this is what happens when taxes are low. Getting rid of poverty is something no government can accomplish by raising taxes and attempting to spread wealth around. Only the private sector can truly and honestly spread wealth by rewarding people for jobs well done. When government officials decide to step in and decide how wealth gets spread, corruption and theft soon make their appearance. As taxes rise across America, people start to hide more and more money some begin breaking the complex federal tax laws to escape the over-taxing powers of the government. The under ground economy also begins to grow as more people use cash to conduct business. Others hire high-priced accountants and lawyers to find ways to hide money.

☐

The latest round of wealth creation happened under George Bush in 2001. When George W. Bush, the 43rd was elected, he took over the presidency in the middle of a mild recession, and his first priority was to CUT TAXES! With just 10 Democrats joining the Republicans, the tax cuts passed the House and was on its way to the Senate for passage. What started out as an $800 billion tax cut by Bush got butchered in the Senate and cut down to just $400 billion before it was passed. This never happens to spending bills in the House or Senate. When they propose a spending bill, it always ends up being a lot larger because greedy politicians stuff their pork in. When it comes to tax cuts, Congress will fight tooth and nail from lowering our taxes; they will not let us have our own money back. Imagine that, the federal government deciding to keep more of OUR MONEY!

After the 2001 tax cuts, we enjoyed seven years of growth and prosperity, unemployment dropped down to 4%, which, statistically, is considered full employment. Even after we were attacked on 911, our economy still recovered and the stock market went on to hit a record high of 14,164. The federal deficit was shrinking month after month. This is the power of tax cuts! To get an idea of why the Bush tax cuts bought unemployment down to 4%, we have to look at how and why tax cuts bring us low unemployment, high stock market values, and prosperity.

□□

What is the difference between the government taxing and taking our money to jumpstart the economy and the government cutting our taxes and letting us decide how to spend the money to jump-start the economy?

When we spend our own money, it is 100% effective in reviving the economy and creating wealth and prosperity. With low taxes, we have more money in our pockets. For example, if you are making $60,000 a year, previously, you paid $20,000 in taxes for an after-tax income of $40,000 to take home and spend on yourself and your family. If, today, the government decided to cut your taxes, and you kept $10,000 more of your money, your after-tax income would be $50,000. What would you do with the extra $10,000 a year? Would you take a vacation across America? If you did it driving, you would spread your $10,000 across this beautiful nation in hotels, convenience stops, parks, thrift shops, and anywhere else you may drive to around the country. This creates jobs across America because you are not the only one driving across the country spending that $10,000. Maybe you would rather remodel your kitchen or bathroom. You will need to hire a contractor and pay for anything construction-related. That contractor will have to go to the hardware store and buy the equipment needed for your remodeling job. It may be a new tile, toilet and faucets, all which have to be manufactured, packaged, delivered and installed. This all contributes to the economy. Many people will give parts of their

$10,000 to charity, which could total into the billions of dollars. Just imagine all that money going into every kind of medical research that people wish to find a cure for. History has shown us over and over that when taxes are low, charitable contributions always reach new highs! This is not government deciding who should get research money, it is decided by the people. And when people decide, most money finds its way to the most important causes. Government always gets it wrong, they end up splurging aid money on wasteful useless programs!

With $10,000 more in our pockets, many of us would also stay local and dine out more often. Who does that help? Restaurant owners, cooks, bartenders, servers, and everyone else who contributes to the restaurant business from the company who delivers and sells the food to the restaurant to the hundreds of different companies manufacturing everything else the restaurants needs to stay in business and serve customers. We can break it down to the advertising and the tooth picks. The point is everything they need has to be manufactured and delivered by people all across the nation. The companies who manufacture these things will need to hire people to work. Now part of our $10,000 trickles down to all these companies that manufacture all these different necessities for the restaurant to function from furniture, flatware, plates, napkins, salt/pepper shakers, and more. Have you ever seen a restaurant supply room? It is filled with hundreds of items, all of which have to be manufactured somewhere. And they also have to be shipped and delivered by someone. As restaurants get busy, they go through these necessities and they have to order more. If you multiply this by 100,000 restaurants across the country, you can get an idea of how all these necessities will be in demand. This is how wealth is spread and jobs are created TAX CUTS!

Many would invest their $10,000 with venture capitalists who take chances on new inventions. Just about everything we have today is because somewhere some venture capitalists took a chance. Whether it was a few hundred dollars or a few hundred million dollars, they took calculated risks like no government ever would. The difference with the risk taking is, when a Venture Cap takes a big risk, they take precautions and extensive research before they invest. The federal government will throw the money behind and idea regardless of outcome.

In the early 1980s, the power of tax cuts gave a boost to the information technology field like no one ever imagined. This incredible technology was integrated into everything from healthcare, construction, and education to advertising, restaurants, travel and much more. When Ronald Reagan cut the top income tax rate from 76% to 28% in the 1980s, our economy started growing rapidly. This was because people suddenly had disposable income to spend. It was clear then, as it is now, if taxes are cut for everyone, we will all end up with more money in our pockets. You can apply the $10,000 in tax savings to just about anything. The bottom line is cutting taxes does create jobs and opportunity to people's lives.

Higher government spending and taxes has always caused high unemployment, higher deficits the destruction of lives and peoples wealth. How is it possible that when government stimulates the economy, we end up with higher unemployment and slow to negative growth? Sometimes government spends so much, we end up in a severe recessions or even a great depression. Make no mistake; the Great Depression was caused directly by the government. When government steps in claiming to prop up the economy and create jobs, hide your wallet! Politicians distribute government money unequally they choose who will get the money and who wont. Sadly, the people getting bailout money are usually lobbyists or special interest groups who did something for the politicians. If we look back at 2008-2009, we can clearly see that the people who got bailout money were banks, lobbyists, union bosses, and environmentalists the very people who gave piles of money to these politicians to get them elected. Federal government bailouts are not to be trusted with politicians. It was the politicians who used our tax dollars to save a field rat, instead of showing some concern for millions of Americans who were one check away from losing their homes.

When we step back and try to make sense of it all, we can all conclude the following. The banks were failing because people no longer had money to pay their bills. This was largely due to the cost of gasoline and energy prices rapidly rising from 2007 to the summer of 2008. This, in essence, was a new gasoline and energy tax on all of us who wake up everyday and go to work. There was no reason for gasoline to go up that high, but Congress did nothing to stop it, and people were squeezed and could not escape this new tax. Many people had to choose whether to pay their mortgage or buy food and gasoline so they could get to work and feed their families. Seeing all this, Congress didn't come to our aid and suggest cutting gasoline taxes. They didn't suggest drilling for more oil on and offshore, Alaska, the Gulf of Mexico, and more. They instead suggested the federal government print trillions of dollars and give much of it to banks.

Because of the government's decision to give money to banks, people didn't have much money to pay mortgages and credit cards. Many jobs are now in jeopardy because the economy slowed down to the point where demand dropped considerably. When the Congress of the United States decided that giving bailout tarp money to banks in 2008 was more important than giving tax cuts to citizens who paid the banks, Congress made a colossal error. They ensured the collapse of the housing market, which is evident in 2009-2010. They also sealed the faith of many businesses causing the loss of millions of jobs. Nancy Pelosi is so incompetent; she has no clue how our economy works. By focusing on banks instead of taxpayers, people ended up losing everything, and banks are still closing all over the country. People now have no money to pay bills, go on vacations, pursue hobbies, or open businesses. The high price of gasoline was a tax, which took over one trillion dollars worth of money out our economy. Taking this much money out the economy is having a catastrophic ripple effect through the US and World economy.

One notable business we all saw close thousands of stores and lay off thousands of employees in the US was Starbucks. Some of you may say, "Who cares, they had overpriced coffee! Close them!" That is a very ignorant and naive way to look at it. If you want to know who cares, how about all the people who were employed by Starbucks? Starbucks created hundreds of thousands of jobs over its years of growth. They created excellent opportunities and touched the lives of thousands of businesses from around the country and around the world. "How?" you may ask. Walk into a Starbucks and look around. Look at everything there, from the windows to the coffee makers to the napkins to the menu to the displays. All these things, these objects, had to be manufactured, delivered, installed, and used for business. The tens of thousands of jobs that Starbucks created were not just for employees of Starbucks. Starbucks helped create jobs for independent contractors, manufacturers, printers, delivery people, farmers, and bakers. You can just list every item down to the tile on the floor. Everything had to be produced, delivered, installed, or assembled, and it was done by a worker who Starbucks had to hire, NOT A GOVERNMENT WORKER! This incredible phenomenon was a result of tax cuts. Because of Bush tax cuts, people had disposable income to pay $8 for a cup of coffee, but that's what freedom is about paying $8 for a cup of coffee that you can get for .95 cents at 7/11. But people wanted more than to just grab a coffee and go; they wanted a place to hang out, sit down, read books, go online, and enjoy the cup of coffee as a reward for their hard work and prosperity. Now, take a business like Starbucks, which, I agree, was a luxury, not a necessity. But that's because I don't work there. For people who were employed by Starbucks, that job was a necessity. You can take Starbucks or look at similar businesses that also fell as a result of this economic mess. You can multiply 10 franchise businesses like Starbucks by thousands of stores failing, and before you know it, you are talking about 2 million lost jobs. This is one example of the damage high gasoline prices caused. This is the proof that Congress, with the leadership of Nancy Pelosi, is a direct cause of our current economic mess. When she consistently ignored the rising price of energy and she purposely did nothing about it, she ensured the demise of thousands of small businesses, thereby sending millions to the unemployment lines.

Having this much power places way too much control over our lives in the hands of one person. The Democrat-run Congress is constantly manipulating and complicating our lives through the tax code. Then, they impose more punishment by raising the taxes, lying, cheating, and telling us we don't pay enough! This is going to go on forever unless we the people stand up to them. Never will you be able to safely and comfortably save for retirement as long as Congress has total control over our wealth and our destiny. Their irresponsible behavior wiped out trillions of dollars worth of wealth in 2 short years. Socialists in Congress created this turbulent environment. There is a way to change this so you never have to worry about Congress destroying our lives and our futures. "How?" you may ask.

One way to take away the destructive powers of Congress is to close the Treasury Department and release all people serving time for tax evasion. Then, we must create a 2% federal sales tax on all goods sold, nothing else! Government does not have the right to tax our services, our paychecks, no FICA or anything that can be used by any single corrupt politician to ruin the lives of millions with the stroke of a pen! If we can get a 2% sales tax on all goods sold in the U.S., the government will never control our lives again. With a 2% federal tax on goods sold and a 75% vote requirement by Congress and Senate to increase it in .5% increments, we could control our destiny once again. It would also take away the power from discriminately taxing our citizens rich or poor. This would create prosperity in the nation like we have never seen before. We would see over $100 trillion worth of economic activity with the IRS out of our lives forever. Every single person in America: visitors, illegals, drug dealers, politicians, pimps, and anyone else who has been eluding the IRS, would now pay the same exact federal taxes that every other honest citizens pay.

Tax cuts should be interpreted as freedom. Money gives us freedom to do whatever we please: take a vacation, buy a car, buy a house, buy a TV, etc. The lower the taxes, the more money the American consumer has in his or her pocket. Therefore, we would have more freedom to choose our own destiny, to move wherever we want to move and to not have to worry about being broke.

As much as the Democratic Party loves to raise your taxes, they sure don't want to pay their own taxes. Many people Barack Obama nominated for posts in his cabinet are tax cheats and tax frauds, yet no one seems to care. By voting for Timothy Geithner, our Congress put an admitted tax cheat in charge of the Department of Treasury (IRS). The corruption on Capitol Hill is one that cannot be allowed to go on; it will doom our future as we know it if we leave it unchecked. We must put an end to TARPs and wasteful government spending. They are taking our tax dollars at a time when we all need it more than ever and they are spreading it irresponsibly. This is what the mafia did by force, and this is what our government is doing. This is how they will keep taking our freedom through our taxes. We need to step up, email, write letters, call, and vote. We must attend tea parties and demand accountability. Trillions of tax dollars are being spent irresponsibly in Washington, D.C. and the only way to take the power back is by demanding that we eliminate all these departments one by one!

Committee on Agriculture

Committee on Appropriations

Committee on Armed Services

Committee on the Budget

Committee on Education and Labor

Committee on Energy and Commerce

Committee on Financial Services

Committee on Foreign Affairs

Committee on Homeland Security

Committee on House Administration

Committee on the Judiciary

Committee on Natural Resources

Committee on Oversight and Government Reform

Committee on Rules

Committee on Science and Technology

Committee on Small Business

Committee on Standards of Official Conduct

Committee on Transportation and Infrastructure

Committee on Veterans' Affairs

Committee on Ways and Means

Joint Economic Committee

Joint Congressional Committee on Inaugural Ceremonies

Trillions of dollars are spent each year, and we have problems with every one of these departments. These departments are like crooked mechanics, we've all seen them or heard of them, the people who keep making our cars worse so we have to keep taking our cars back to them. Now we have to pay even more to fix it again and we keep coming back because we have to fix it again because it's broken again because it has to be fixed again! Does that sound insane? That is how insane our federal government has become. It is not going to affect our lives negatively if we eliminate each and every one of those departments; that is 100% FACT! If we get rid of those departments one by one, the government will remove a layer of taxes for each department closed. All of those savings would create growth and prosperity like we had in the 1980s and 2000. The extra revenue generated will help the government balance its budget. With millions of new jobs across the country, every sector in our lives will improve not just in America but also all over the world. It is simply amusing to watch ignorant Americans believe in politicians who talk of how government will create jobs and fix everything. REALLY? After 13 trillion dollars wasted and over 10% unemployment rate, who can honestly believe that the federal government will fix anything? ☐When George W. Bush cut taxes, we didn't need any federal government agency to help create jobs, we didn't need any TARP or Bailout Money to create jobs all we needed were tax cuts!

We should all demand Congress close the Department of Treasury and enact a 2% federal sales tax. That's it— no more IRS, no more April 15! With no more than a 2% federal tax from the US government and eventually all federal departments shut down or audited, we would not see recessions for the rest of our lives! With no departments, one person in congress will no longer be able to decide our energy policy or our education among other things. Don't believe their class envy; to get our freedom back we need to take the power out of the hands of socialists in government. We can't eliminate socialists completely they will be with us forever, we can however take away the tools, tools which socialists use against us. These tools are the federal departments politicians have created. If we don't shut down these departments, we will win small battles by stopping bills or slowing down the federal government but that will just be a temporary fix to our ongoing problems. Once things settle back down, people forget and new socialists will be elected, then the government will be right back with the same exact ideas and goals of more federal control over our lives. This is evident with the Universal Health Care Bill, the federal government has been trying to control health care for over 50years now. The evil corruption of our government will not stop unless we stop it! Just like when America rejected Hillary Clinton's Socialized Healthcare in 1993, socialists did not quit, they stayed and waited to fight another day. Now we are at that day and they are attacking from all sides. Nancy Pelosi and the rest of the socialists are attempting to accomplish what Hillary Clinton Failed at! The only way we can stop them from planning and scheming like this is to WIN THE

WAR! To win the WAR, we must demand that congress shut down each department one by one starting with the Department of Energy. If we can accomplish closing departments, we will win the WAR against destructive politicians who have been manipulating our lives for over 100 years!

Chapter 8 – United Nations

"Organizations that elevate dictators, socialists, and warlords are doomed for failure"

After the catastrophic failure of the League of Nations (1919–1946), which the United States never joined, the United Nations was formed in 1945. Their purpose was similar to that of the League of Nations, which was to maintain international peace and promote cooperation in solving international economic, social, and humanitarian problems. Sixty years later, like the League of Nations, the United Nations turned out to be a catastrophic failure and disappointment as well. Under the watchful eyes of the League of Nations, WWII broke out. Under the United Nations, WWIII broke out. Today America and the world are fighting extremist Muslims all over the World.

The earliest plan for the United Nations was started under the oversight of the U.S. State Department in 1939. Franklin D. Roosevelt first coined the term 'United Nations' when describing the Allied countries. On January 1, 1942, when 26 governments signed the Atlantic Charter pledging to continue the war efforts, the foundation for the UN was established. On the 25th of April, 1945 the UN Conference on International Organization started in San

Francisco, there were 50 governments in attendance and a few of non-governmental organizations involved in drafting the Charter of the United Nations. The UN officially came into existence on October 24, 1945 upon ratification of the Charter by the five permanent members of the Security Council France, the Republic of China, the Soviet Union, the United Kingdom, and the United States and by a majority of the other 46 signatories.

It didn't take long for the United Nations to prove itself to be as useless as the League of Nations in the past. From their inception to the present time, the UN has been littered with corruption and lies. The UN's reputation was tarnished in 2003 after the Oil-for-Food scandal was exposed. The program was established in 1996 to allow Iraq to sell oil on the world market in exchange for food, medicine, and other humanitarian supplies. This program was meant for Iraqi citizens who were affected by international economic sanctions in the wake of the first Gulf War. Allegations of abuse and corruption surfaced in 2003. The former director Benon Sevan was suspended and then resigned from the UN. It was proven beyond a reasonable fact that he was found to have accepted bribes from the Iraqi regime. He put his own self-interest ahead of the hungry children in the world. Benon Sevan stuffed his pockets with money just to let a brutal terrorist get his way. He never gave back the money he took as a bribe. It was recommended that his UN immunity be lifted to allow for a criminal investigation. Beyond Sevan, Kojo Annan, Kofi Annan's son, also engaged in corruption in the Oil-for-Food contracts on behalf of the Swiss company Cotecna. All this happened while his father, Kofi Annan, was UN Secretary

General. Corruption must run in the family. They were not the only corrupt people associated with the UN. India's foreign minister, K. Natwar Singh, was removed from office because of a role in the scandal, and the Cole Inquiry investigated whether the Australian Wheat Board breached any laws with its contracts with Iraq. The United Nation does not care about the world. If you really want to grade them, I would give them an F and take away all their privileges.

Have they had any great achievements since they have been around? During the UN's existence, Communist Russia became stronger than ever. It took an American president to begin the fall of the great soviet Empire. The UN just idly watched and did nothing while it was happening. It took America about 35 years to bring down the great Evil Soviet Empire. Berlin was split into two separate cities with people risking their lives to get across the old Berlin wall. Many were shot and killed! The UN did not condemn the communists. In Cambodia, the UN stood by as communists murdered millions in the late 1970s. It was the same with Vietnam, North Korea, Sudan, Rwanda, and any other country that was overtaken by communists or dictators. The United Nations does not care!

Today, like in the past, the world is filled with murder, mayhem, rape, massacre, conspiracies and theft of public funds. The rule of powerful tyrannical kings, dictators, warlords, and many other conceited corrupt leaders around the world. Just like in the past, today, there are many who rule over their people with no respect for the Peoples individual rights. Life is difficult, brutal, and unfair in most of the world, yet the UN does nothing about it. Just like in the past, still today the rule of law ends at the tip of the most powerful individual's gun, depending on where on earth you happen to live. It is sad and true that in many nations around the world, people still live under this kind of oppression in the 21st century! The United Nations whole purpose is to stop this kind of brutal rule of nations over their citizens around the world. They are supposed to be in Afghanistan exterminating the Taliban, Al-Qaeda and other terrorists. They should be in North Korea with the support of the rest of the world to remove Kim Jong-Ill. They should be in Myanmar disarming the military. Don't hold your breath; the UN is not going to do anything to stop these evil dictators in poor nations.

The problem with the UN is they don't care about poor nations. The diplomats at the United Nations look at a nation's wealth, and if the nation has nothing to offer to the UN, then the UN does not care to help or do anything for them. This is why they are centered in New York and not Sudan or Rwanda! Would Africa be such a dangerous continent if the United Nations were headquartered in the most dangerous spot there? They are the United Nations; they took an oath to make the world a better place and stand up for poor people around the world. They should be forced out of the United Nations building in New York and we should build them a hut in Rwanda, Sudan, or Afghanistan. Let's see the UN work on making the world a safer place. It's obvious that by being headquartered in NYC, all they are doing is wasting time and American taxpayer money. The world is falling apart and they accomplish nothing, and to top it off, they are always demanding for more money from America. All around us in the world we see chaos, the poor being mistreated, and unstable nations building WMDs (weapons of mass destruction). Instead, the UN looks at the United States and Israel as the cause of all the problems of the world.

IN 2003, the UN decided to elect Libya to chair the United Nations Human Rights Commission, despite opposition from the United States. This is ludicrous; to choose a nation which commits human rights abuses and violations to oversee and stomp out human rights abuses is like appointing a serial rapist as the dean of an all-girls school. Its eerily similar to when the UN stood by as the aggressive evil Communist Soviet Empire decided to invade neighboring countries in the 1950s. The UN made a colossal error by allowing communist Soviet Union sit on the Security Council. Their position in the Security Council allowed the Soviets to override any attempts to stop communist invasion of peaceful Nations all over the world.

It is sad and true; the United Nations has caused more harm than good, and at the same time, they've wasted hundreds of billions of dollars. Some of this money has been used for helping terrorists. Since inception, the UN has meddled in the Middle East in the 1940s, in North Korea in the 1950s, and in Europe and Asia. The results of their meddling are still noticeable. North Korea is a jail for millions of citizens living under oppressive rule of Kim Jong Ill. Tensions in the Middle East are rising and on the verge of a nuclear holocaust. Europe has finally shed the evil grip of communism but the UN had no role in it! So what is the UN up to? They are in the process of limiting the productivity of western nations. Using manipulated and faulty data, the UN would like tax carbon emissions and energy usage. This is the United Nation's first priority! Putting an end to genocide, war, murder, hunger, or diseases gets lost in the corruption at the UN. Instead, these powerful world leaders choose to enforce a global hoax and create more poverty around the world.

The UN does have a lot of valuable important people, they are the ones who work out in the field the doctors, the social workers, the people who are in the middle of it all. These are the people treating the sick, educating the children, and helping build a safe and functioning society in broken nations. As the people on the ground do their jobs in the third world countries and filing reports, the UN diplomats take whatever progress is being made and they destroy it in the blink of an eye. This usually happens when field agents file an unfavorable report, and the diplomats sweep it under the rug because of associations with the powerful oppressors in those nations.

The problem with the UN is they really don't have the power to enforce anything, so they are of no threat to any nation on earth. Saddam Hussein discovered this early on, that is why he broke all the UN resolutions. He knew the UN would not enforce them. They showed how useless they were when UN troops were assaulted by a pack of kids with machine guns in Mogadishu. Instead of fighting and disarming, the UN packed up and retreated. With guns and threats, warlords take what they want, and the UN, with all their weapons and training, do absolutely nothing. As long as this is the case, whatever country the UN works in will kick all aid workers out if they see fit. There is also a lot of corruption behind the scenes that really discourages any changes to the troubled nations they are trying to help. At the diplomatic level, the UN is as corrupt as a third world country run by a dictator like Castro, Chavez, or Kim Jong-Ill. There are bribes, deals, and behind-the-scenes backroom agreements, which set back any progress. If the UN were actually effective, why is it that wherever they attempt to fix problems, soon, more severe problems follow?

In the 1950s North Korea invaded South Korea, the UN rushed to South Korea's aid only to fall back when the Chinese gave reinforcements to North Korea. The UN was powerless and needed more help; the United States military came to the rescue of South Korea, and helped secure the border at the 38th parallel. To this day, North and South Korea still have not signed a cease-fire pact or peace treaty. Technically, they are still at war. The UN was ineffective at convincing the Chinese not to help the North. The UN was ineffective at convincing both Koreas to work out a peace treaty. The UN was ineffective at protecting the innocent all over the world.

Again, the UN showed how truly useless they are in Europe. In the year 1956, the communist Soviet Union invaded Hungary. The UN called upon the Soviets to withdraw right away. Fortunately, the Soviet Union happened to be on the UN Security Council and simply vetoed the UN's request to withdraw from Hungary. Thanks to the incompetence of the UN, tens of millions of innocent people became slaves of the Soviet Empire. The UN did nothing to reverse this. Just whom are they helping?

Again, in the 1970s, with the killing fields in Cambodia and all the atrocities in South-east Asia thanks to the spread of communism. The UN did nothing to stop it or to bring the world's attention to the killing of millions of innocent women, children, and men all over Asia.

In the 1980s, in Somalia and Central America, as dictators and warlords were oppressing people around the world, the UN was busy racking up parking tickets in New York City. While the UN members partied like rock stars and cost us billions of dollars, freedom for the oppressed around the world became a fading dream.

In 1994, there was genocide in Rwanda where hundreds of thousands of innocent people were butchered with blunt machetes. To get an idea of where the priorities of the UN lay, during the genocide in Rwanda, instead of dealing with this atrocity, the UN ignored the outcries for help and went on with business as if everything were fine. They even had time for a champagne and caviar party in South Africa while just 3,000 miles North; thousands of people's heads were chopped off with blunt machetes. Some say, "Its Africa; nobody cares." This is how socialists and dictators value life. They simply don't care; this just proves that the UN is useless.

One would expect that by the year 2000, they would have gotten it right, yet the UN still stands by while human rights are being denied all over the world. Instead of investigating serious offenders, they find it important to focus on the United States' treatment of terrorists. There are people being murdered, tortured, and starved yet the UN finds it convenient to accuse America of torture in Guantanamo Bay. The terrorists in American prisons get three full-course meals prepared by a chef. They get to choose their dinners off a menu! Why is the UN not focusing on Iran's treatment of political prisoners? The prisoners who are fortunate to survive the torture they are subjected to by Iranian secret police. One of the darkest moments in the UN's history which was alarming is when Hugo Chavez gave a speech to the UN, many of the members were cheering and clapping for him while he was insulting president George W. Bush. The reason this was alarming is that Hugo Chavez is a dictator who oppresses free people in his nation. He is doing to Venezuela what President Obama is trying to accomplish in the United States. Hugo Chavez is taking over every private industry and injecting government control into every aspect of the people's lives in Venezuela. He has closed down TV stations and confiscated oil companies, hotels, and anything else he sets his eyes on. This is what President Obama is yearning for. This is not what President George W. Bush was for. As the UN cheers on Hugo Chavez, it shows the corrupt and evil mentality of the people who make up the United Nations assembly.

The UN has become an obstructive bureaucracy; they get in the way of the poor nations, which need the assistance, and the wealthy nations that are willing to help. Instead of a well-run organization whose interests are to help deprived nations and help the helpless, they have become politicians wasting valuable resources. In some countries, the so-called UN peacekeepers were raping underage children in Africa and selling the rape videos on the Internet. This scandal rocked the UN so hard that Kofi Annan nearly resigned. With the rape scandal and Kojo Annan (Kofi's son) involved in the Oil-for-Food Scandal, the UN was losing what little credibility it had left.

Today, we can see the UN spreading climate change propaganda and attempting to regulate energy use. If the past is any indication of the future, the UN is not going to change its ways. In fact, they will keep following their current ways while the world keeps falling into deeper chaos with more dictators and communists taking power. These people are also pursuing WMDs and total control over their populations. Like in the 1960s when the Soviets vetoed the UN resolution to withdraw from Hungary, these people are giving themselves the green light to roll over any country they felt like. The UN member nations today still practice these tactics. Before the invasion of Iraq, France, Germany, and Russia repeatedly tried blocking the United States from passing a resolution to form a coalition to invade Iraq. Repeatedly through the past 50 years, the UN has made things worse and has kept America back from helping millions of innocent nations. There has to be a better solution to the problems of the world, as it is painfully obvious that the UN is not doing its job. Over one billion people on this planet are living with no rights because their government oppresses them. The UN should recognize this and make the necessary changes to ensure everyone has equal rights all around the World.

The United Nations is creating an atmosphere where leaders around the world shy away from freedom and truth and lean towards socialism, oppression and corruption. Bush did his best to show the world that America was an honest nation ruled by law, not by corrupt politicians. Unfortunately, the Democrats ruined everything by bending laws and creating an atmosphere of corruption. The election of Barack Obama told the world that the United States is not serious about fighting evil around the world. Today, powerful leaders like Vladmir Putin in Russia are befriending people like Hugo Chavez. Hugo Chavez has dinner with Iranian Leader Mahmoud Ahmadinejad and Cuban leader Fidel Castro. These ruthless leaders live above the laws of their nations and are organizing and conspiring against America. The trail is clear and it's in front of us; evil is gaining strength and our president or the United nations are not doing anything to slow it down or stop it!

Chapter 9 – Solutions

"We can only reach utopia if we are all free to contribute to society in our own way; we can only contribute to society in our own way if we are not forced to contribute in their way!"

T he United States is in a $13 trillion-dollar hole and it's sinking fast. How do we fix this giant mess? Today, congress is wrecking finance, healthcare, energy, manufacturing and just about every part of our economy. Soon, all Americans will start to feel the evil grip of socialism/communism and realize how destructive the federal government has become. We will see this via long unemployment lines, more foreclosures and more people on welfare. Most of this is happening because people are not paying attention to what our leaders are doing. The federal government is consistently making life more difficult for us, and forcing us to do irrational things. As time goes on government is complicating the tax laws, making our health care even more complex and expensive, making payrolls, taxes and commerce more difficult all across America. Through control of the energy department alone, government forces us more taxes upon us. They involve themselves in issues like healthcare, sports steroids and countless meetings, which serve no purpose and have nothing to do with national security, creating jobs, or helping people stay in their homes. Our federal government has corrupted unions, banks, and other organizations. We are no longer in control of our own destiny; we are now becoming a slave to the system, the system of government we trusted evolved into an out of control monster right in front of us. By not paying attention to what the politicians have been doing and are doing in Washington, we are letting them take full control of our futures, our health, our retirement, our savings, our education, and our cost of living. They have proven repeatedly that they are not responsible enough to manage any of those things.

There is a solution. It's a simple one, and many people will oppose it. This solution may seem too good to be true at first, which it is, possibly because things have become so complex that doing this one thing seems too logical and simple. The truth is to solve our problems, all we have to do is unite and demand the federal government close a department every couple of months. How would this help people? How would it make life better for you and I if there were no Department of Energy or Federal Environmental Protection Agency? It would make life better in many ways, when the Department of Energy is closed, the positive affects will be felt in every state from Hawaii to Alaska to Florida and Maine. People will see the price of gasoline heating oil and electricity drop substantially, by over 50% in many cases. This will happen because the department of energy is no longer going to be under the control of one person telling states what they can or can't do. This means 50 states will now be in control of their destiny, they will have the power to build power plants, drill for oil, mine for coal and bring us more clean affordable energy which does not destroy the planet.

With these 50 states creating new sources of energy, we will see businesses once again stat to pick up steam due to the low price of energy. This would create more jobs, REAL JOBS, not the phony government jobs, it would also put more money in peoples pockets. The ripple affect of cheap energy will spread across America like a title wave of prosperity. Jobs will be created by the hundreds of thousands monthly and people will once again have incomes to pay mortgages and credit cards. This in turn will get banks to be more trust worthy and start lending money again. Closing the Department of Energy and other departments will also get lobbyists out of Washington D.C. Because of the Department of Energy, our gasoline costs thrice as much as it would if the Department of Energy had never existed. With gasoline around $1 a gallon, people will have extra disposable money in their pockets, money to spend going out and consuming.

The Energy Department was created in 1977 and it should be abolished in 2010. This department has proven to be more harmful and devastating to the US economy than any other department. It is true we had an oil embargo around the time the Department was created, but the solution was not to make it more difficult for Americans to drill for their own oil when the world was keeping oil from us on purpose, yet that is exactly what congress did! When there was a shortage in oil, congress didn't send out government officials to give us more energy, they instead created a government agency, which restricted energy. Congress has created this department and granted themselves over one trillion dollars worth of control in our economy and our lives.

Once we close the Department of Energy, we will enjoy a tremendous boost to our economy. No longer will states be forced to accept House Speaker Nancy Pelosi's socialist ideologies, which have overtaken the Congress of the United States and brought us to the recession of 2009. The steps to take our freedom back must be taken by the people. We can't wait for elected officials to come along and make things happen. It has been proven that great leaders come along occasionally, and they give us a few years of prosperity and freedom. Then a few short years later, we end up giving all back to a new breed of greedy politicians. It happened with Reagan. When Jimmy Carter lost the election, our nation was sliding deep into recession; Ronald Reagan came along, cut taxes, and lifted us out of the horrible mess Jimmy Carter left us. Now, just 20 short years after Reagan left office, the Democrats are trying to push the taxes back up towards the 76% that Jimmy Carter left us with. They are also creating new government agencies and bureaucracies; this is why leaders will never solve our problems, its like trying to cure your alcoholism by drinking a bottle of Scotch! The only way we can permanently solve our problems is if we, as citizens, unite and demand that the federal government shut down every single department, one by one.

☐

The only new department we need to create is a department to close down all Federal Departments. This could be done in a timely manner and the ripple affect it will have in our lives will give us more advancements in a short period of time than ever before in human civilizations. A closed federal departments leaves the politicians with nothing to do so they can stop wasting our time and money in Washington D.C. They were not elected to be full time law makers writing laws and regulations day after day.

Another brilliant fair and just solution is to take away the pension and any other government provided benefits from every retired member of congress and senate. These are the leaders of yesterday, they have destroyed our future, and they should not be rewarded with benefits, which are paid by the American Tax Payer. 100% of their estate should be confiscated once they expire for they have driven our nation into a $13 trillion debt. Once the $13 trillion debt is satisfied, they can receive their pensions.

These are not huge tasks, if we look at history and the sacrifices people made for this country, getting a few million Americans to march on Washington D.C. And demand congress shut down the department of Energy can happen. It's up to us to make it happen like great leaders made things happen for us. George Washington crossed the Delaware River with a hand full of freedom-loving militia that was barely an army. These brave men rowed their boats across a freezing cold river with chunks of ice floating around them in the cold dark winter night because they wanted to be free. These young men were freezing and had rags wrapped around their feet to keep them warm; freezing their tails off, they were going into an uncertain battle where they were likely to be killed. Many people risked their lives for liberty under brutal conditions and American always prevailed thanks to all the named and unnamed heroes who made this country so great. □We are a nation of heroes waiting for our moment, waiting for our time.

Our government can work for us if the evil powers of corruption can be removed from the grip of life long politicians. With no federal control over energy, education, food and interest rates, states can regulate and decide on their own what they want. With the corrupt and thick layer of the federal government removed from our lives, politicians will no longer have any tools to manipulate our wealth. With no departments in our lives, congress and senate will once again represent the people and ensure that no federal departments will ever be created!

The candidate who will fight for the American people will say these simple words! "Mr President! Tear Down This Department!" Everyone will cheer and get behind this candidate because that is what we all want! Freedom from government oppression.

Visit www.destructivepolitics.com to email Congress. Let's make a difference.

- Notes -

Visit www.destructivepolitics.com for all relevant footnotes, news
articles, video clips and other related information.

www.ingramcontent.com/pod-product-compliance
Lightning Source LLC
Chambersburg PA
CBHW021604280526
45784CB00001BA/489